D1490350

SURFING

THE ULTIMATE PLEASURE

For Nedra, Lorca and Asia

_____

Copyright © 1984 by Leonard Lueras

All rights reserved. No portion of this book may be reproduced
— mechanically, electronically, or by any other means, including
photocopying — without written permission of the publisher.
Published simultaneously in Canada by Saunders of Toronto, Inc.

Library of Congress Cataloging in Publication Data

Lueras, Leonard
   Surfing, The Ultimate Pleasure.

   Discography: p.
   Filmography: p.
   Bibliography: p.
   Includes Index.
   1. Surfing.   2. Surfing — United States — History.   I. Title.
GV840.S8L84   1984   797.1'72   83-40541
ISBN 0-89480-749-8 (Workman)
ISBN 0-89480-708-0 (Workman: pbk.)

Cover and Book Design: Fred Bechlen
Front Cover Photograph: Aaron Chang
Back Cover Photograph: Stephen O. Muskie
Front Flap Photograph: ca. 1890, by Theodore Severin,
   from the Bernice Pauahi Bishop Museum
Frontispiece: Detail, 'Surfing at Hilo Bay,'
   ca. 1850, Artist Unknown

An Emphasis International Book

Workman Publishing
1 West 39 Street
New York, NY 10018

Manufactured in Hong Kong
Printed by Toppan Printing Company (HK) Ltd
First Printing March 1984

10 9 8 7 6 5 4 3 2 1

SURFING

THE ULTIMATE PLEASURE

WRITTEN AND PRODUCED BY LEONARD LUERAS
DESIGNED BY FRED BECHLEN

AN EMPHASIS INTERNATIONAL BOOK

WORKMAN PUBLISHING
NEW YORK

CONTENTS

8   DROPPING IN

12   HE'ENALU

30   LYRICAL POLYNESIAN ORIGINS
An early history of surfing as recounted in fascinating chants passed down by early Hawaiians. The importance of *he'enalu* in the day-to-day and diplomatic life of commoners and royalty of the Hawaiian Islands.

46   'A MOST SUPREME PLEASURE'
Beginning with Captain James Cook, early and later *haole* are 'stoked' by what they see happening offshore. Log entries by navigators-explorers, and charming, poetic observations by visiting writers such as Lord Byron, Mark Twain and literary others.

68   ON THE BEACH AT WAIKIKI
The world's first two surf clubs are organized just after the turn-of-the-century and ancient surfing enjoys a much-needed 'renaissance' in the form of earnest 'Western' surfers and a new breed of sports and fun-loving locals called 'beachboys.' A surfside society evolves.

88   THE DUKE: SURFING'S 'FATHER'
Duke Kahanamoku, the most famous and honored 'water man' in Hawaiian history, introduces surfing and Hawaii to the outside world after achieving fame as the fastest swimmer in the world. Initiates in California and Australia listen to The Duke's instructions and surfing takes off in those well-waved places.

104   A CULT IS BORN
California-style surfing begins its curious development. The first modern-era pioneers paddle furiously, form surf clubs, design new watercraft, and initiate virgin surf spots. Palos Verdes, Malibu and San Onofre are where it's at.

124   THE SIXTIES: 'SURFING U.S.A.'
Anybody worth a good ding or two heads for 'Surf City.' Woodies line beaches and bluffs at Malibu, Doheny and Crystal Pier. Gremmies, Kooks, Greasers and Locals collide. The Surfer Stomp marks time. Cowabunga! stoke! and fascinating surfcetera.

144   SURF CHIC
Surfing influences fashion, music, dance, language and youthful lifestyle in general. Surf shops, surf art, surf flicks, surf magazines and surf stars develop. The blonde, California surfer look makes trendy waves.

162 PROFESSIONALS CASH IN
Surfers 'unionize', fraternize and advertise.
Sponsors who wish to capitalize on the sport's
glamour dangle big bucks and motion picture
cameras in front of surfing's thoroughbreds.

168 KA NALU

188 WAVES FROM ABROAD
In their never-ending quest for The Perfect
Wave, surfers become purposeful travelers.
From Niijima to St. Jean de Luz, and from the
cliffs of Cornwall to the jungles of Java, the
surfer draws oohing and ahhing crowds.

200 'WINDSURFING' TAKES OFF
A new surfing pastime, 'windsurfing,' sweeps
the world. Many longtime surfers try out this
new sports cousin and are once again 'stoked.'
Sailing surfboards soar to new heights.

202 APPENDICES

204 EVOLUTION OF THE SURFBOARD
Templates and descriptions of surfing
gear — from ancient waveriding times to the
technological present.

210 SURF MUSIC
A selected discography of out-of-print and
available surf music LPs.

216 A SURF FILMOGRAPHY
From Thomas A. Edison to 'Blazing Boards,'
a year-by-year listing of proper surf films and
films that include surfing or are about surfing.

222 BIBLIOGRAPHY
An annotated, alphabetical (by author)
compilation of written surfing sources, popular
and academic, fiction and non-fiction.

229 INDEX

233 CREDITS/ACKNOWLEDGMENTS

"Do you remember your first wave? The first time you stood up and actually surfed?"

When an old friend asked that question recently, my mind filled with wonder and nostalgia. Our cocktail conversation blurred, some 25 years rinsed away, and I was 13 years old again.

It was the summer of '59, and the place, as I recall, was Doheny Beach in south Orange County. Like many another Southern California *gremmie* who hung out at the beach, I was floundering around in Doheny's benign whitewater, awkwardly, nay desperately, trying to catch that elusive first wave. "Outside," in the fast-breaking "Boneyard," the *real* surfers were left-go-righting, cutting back, climbing and dropping — "hotdogging" they called it then — and their prowess only added to my "inside" embarrassment.

But finally, somehow, God granted me and my badly dinged Velzy our wish. I didn't fall; the board didn't *pearl*; and together we didn't — as they say in Hawaii — make ass. Instead, we slid forward with a swell, began maintaining an improbable kinetic energy all our own, and, for the first time, I stood up and moved into a new and exhilarating world that has held me transfixed ever since.

"Do you remember your first wave?"

It's not a profound question. I mean, it's not like asking you to recall your first orgasm. Or asking where you were when Kennedy was shot. But that simple line — *"Do you remember your first wave?"* — evokes a curious, warm feeling.

Hundreds of waves and four years after that first ride, this time in soft Hawaiian waters, the meaning, importance and sheer joy of waveriding was yet again amplified. It was June of '63, and a California friend and I were on a first time pilgrimage to Hawaii "to surf." We arrived in Honolulu at nightfall, bummed a ride from the airport into Waikiki, and checked into a cheap "Jungle" bungalow. At dawn the next morning we carried our boards nearly the length of Waikiki Beach and paddled out to the famous Ala Moana surfing break under the grey-pink of first light.

The waves didn't look very big from the breakwater, but as we made our way out through the Ala Wai Harbor's boat channel, we watched big-eyed as a long-haired Hawaiian in red baggy trunks dropped into a swell that had lifted above Ala Moana's outside marker poles. We coast *haole* were honestly terrified by the beauty, motion and power of an overhead Hawaiian wave.

As that local boy casually disappeared into a warm aqua tunnel, another Hawaiian yelled loudly: "Go Hawaii! Go!"

"Hawaii" went, and a moment later he emerged from a crushing but pure Ala Moana tube. As his ride ended, he kicked out in a neat standing up position, tore at his dark hair with both hands, and screamed a primeval scream. In approving response, a chorus of surfer hoots filled the balmy air. "Hawaii" was stoked, our minds were blown, and nothing else in the world mattered during that moment of pure, euphoric rebirth. Except, perhaps, the next, outside wave . . . .

Do you remember your first tube ride?

Since ancient Polynesian times, centuries before boogie boards and pocket rockets, surfers have tried to explain to non-surfers why their sport has such a hypnotic hold on them. But as many are fond of saying, "It's like trying to explain sex to a virgin."

"Why," an elderly journalist friend asked recently, "do I see these young fellows arriving here at the beach every morning when it's still dark? They sit in their cars until the sun rises, then go out and surf for hours without coming in. Later, another group arrives and they stay out in the water until you can barely see them in the twilight. What is there about this sport that makes obvi-ously healthy and sane people do such things — sometimes every day for a week or so?"

The answers to such questions are as varied — and poetic — as waves breaking on a jagged reef.

Paul Strauch, long one of Hawaii's most-respected champion surfers and now a conscientious businessman who surfs "for relaxation," revives the sexual simile. "Surfing," he says, "is very much like making love. It always feels good — no matter how many times you've done it. But what is most important about surfing — as with loving — is its worth to the individual. There's a strong sense of fulfillment — as opposed to frustration."

Some surfer types are not so eloquent. Jeff Spicoli, the San Diego surfer-doper in Cameron Crowe's fine 1981 novel *Fast Times at Ridgemont High*, proclaims in his Universal movie role: "There's only two things I want out of life. Some tasty waves and a righteous buzz."

Meanwhile, high atop Los Angeles' Times-Mirror Square, at the epicenter of Southern California media power, yet another surfer, Times-Mirror chairman Otis Chandler, waxes metaphysical.

Surfing, Chandler says of his favorite sport, "is an individual expression of one's own worth and one's own ability to participate directly with nature. And what makes it really enjoyable to me is that every wave is different . . . there's a special, non-repetitive pleasure in it that never gets boring."

Chandler said during a recent interview in his office that he's been addicted to waveriding since 1937 ("I was about 10 years old then"), the year his father bought him a six foot lemonwood, balsa and redwood surfboard manufactured by California's then Swastika Surfboard Company. Since his childhood Thirties, he has grown with the sport and its changing technology, despite a heavy business schedule and the fact that few of his publishing and chronological peers surf.

"Professionally," Chandler says, "I'm looked

At left, a loinclothed surfer and family pose outside their grass beach home. This fine documentary photo, ca. 1890, was art-directed and shot by Theodore P. Severin. It is in the photo archives of the Bernice Pauahi Bishop Museum, Honolulu.

Two North Shore surfers-in-residence punch over the top and scramble for position during a recent "masters" competition at Oahu's Banzai Pipeline.

upon as kind of a crazy because I surf, ride dirt bikes, ride street bikes, race Porsches and hunt." But the physical and "spiritual" rewards, he says, make his "craziness" worthwhile. He likens surfing, for example, to a religious experience.

"I'm not a church-goer. I believe in God, Christian-type," Chandler says, "but sometimes when I'm surfing, particularly when I'm by myself, on a good day . . . I feel very close to God."

Another publisher-surfer, Steve Pezman, the longtime editorial director of *Surfer* magazine, says that "surfing is a very personal thing. Even if you're surfing in a crowd, you're by yourself. You're always one on one with the wave, no matter how many people are out there." But more important, Pezman said, "the act of surfing is a special form of interaction with life. Each wave is a life unit, and when you learn to flow gracefully with a wave, you're learning to flow with life."

Dave Rochlen, a Honolulu surfing wear manufacturer (Surfline Hawaii) and an early and well-known Santa Monica-Malibu local, attributes surfing's popularity to man's natural awe and respect for the sea. "It's simple," he says. "The ocean is the most wondrous thing on our planet, and the breaking wave is the single most exciting thing happening in the ocean. And perhaps the strongest thing you can say about surfing is that it allows you, like nearly nothing else does, the excitement of playing with the ocean. No other sport gives you such an immediate, exciting and fulfilling feedback.

"It's like going down to the sea—'men of ships' stuff. Like when you're young, and caught inside on a ten foot day, you become part of a cadre of special forces. What's that poem about a British RAF chap reaching out and touching the face of God? It's something like that. There's something about the ocean, this mother surf monster, and the way she can control and tease you. And to be into surfing—that is, to be a surfer—is to be part of a very serious cult. It's a form of religion, based on a special relationship with nature."

Duke Boyd, who over the years has developed the very successful Hang Ten and Lightning Bolt surfing lines, identifies with surfing's "wild and isolated feeling." He relates to surfing as an "art form" or "waterborne ballet."

"In its early modern days, surfing was considered a sport. Not organized, but a sport. But in the early Sixties it began to be recognized as having a soul. Then, with the advent of lighter and more maneuverable balsa and foam boards, we began to see surfing as an art form," Boyd said.

"Do you remember," Boyd was asked, *"your first wave?"*

A smile crossed Boyd's face, and a certain naive enthusiasm swelled within him. "Yeah," he sighed, "those were the days when you were truly in love with nature. You'd stand on the beach at the end of a long day of surfing and your arms would hurt, you'd be burnt, your hair would be a little more blond, and there'd be some more dings on your board. You'd stand there dead tired, but you'd still say, 'God, if I had enough strength, I'd go out again.'"

This seemingly irrational dedication and euphoria is not a newly nihilistic phenomenon perpetrated by 20th Century "beach bums." Even Hawaiian chants of the 16th and 17th centuries tell of surfing days when surfers would leave everything behind—work, family, everything—to ride waves and place wagers on favored surfers. When the surf is up, recalled the 19th Century Hawaiian scholar Kepelino Keauokalani, "All thought of work is at an end, only that of sport is left . . . All day there is nothing but surfing. Many go out surfing as early as four in the morning."

The British explorer Captain James Cook, the first Westerner to describe surfing, took particular note of this obsession. In a 1777 ship's log entry, he observed that Polynesian surfers could care less about the mysterious foreigners in their midst when indulging in their favorite sport. Noting the romance inherent in this fascinating pastime, he compared the flowing effects of surfing to the soothing feelings one experiences when listening to classical music.

What, one wonders, would a visiting extraterrestrial think of this high physics phenomenon were he to accidentally land his spacecraft on Oahu's North Shore on a particularly fine surfing day? Would a Venutian or Martian marvel at this recreational use of natural energy vectors?

Whatever the reason for surfing's grip on hundreds of thousands of people, one thing is certain: The sport has grown and continues to grow, phenomenally. Since Hawaiians first introduced their sport to the U.S. Mainland and Australia early in this century, the image of *the surfer* has been adopted as an "unofficial" state and national symbol. And in purely economic terms, surfing-related products have become part of a billion dollars a year industry. The surfer "look" has become not just a frivolous fad, but has evolved into a staying, fashionable trend (some call it a "lifestyle") that has become even more pervasive and important with the recent popularization of a new sister sport called boardsailing or windsurfing.

The real bottom waveline, however, is still a simple, soothing and rhythmic concept that has to do with paddling out into an open space, "getting wet," and losing oneself in a pulsing, saltwater sea. It's a remembrance of waves past, waves ridden and the projection of one's mind and body into waves still unknown.

Indeed, ask any surfer that simple question — *"Do you remember your first wave?"* — and you'll soon find out why we're still stoked — after all these years.

HE'ENALU

he'e nalu. To ride a surfboard; surfing; surf rider. *Lit.*, wave sliding.

he'e. To slide, surf, slip, flee.

nalu. Wave, surf; full of waves; to form waves; wavy, as wood grain. *Ke nalu nei ka moana,* the ocean is full of waves.

— from Samuel Elbert and Mary Kawena Pukui's
Hawaiian Dictionary, *Honolulu, 1971.*

Heenalu (he'e-na'-lu), n. [Hee and nalu, the surf.]

Hee (he'e), n. 1. A flowing, as of liquid. 2. The menses. 3. A flight, as of a routed army. 4. The squid, so-called from his slippery qualities.

Hee (he'e), v. 1. To melt; to run or flow, as a liquid. 2. To slip or glide along. 3. To ride on a surfboard. 4. To flee; to flee through fear.

Nalu (na'-lu), adj. Roaring; surfing; rolling in, as the surf of the sea.

Nalu (na'-lu), n. 1. The surf as it rolls in upon the beach; a sea; a wave; a billow. 2. The slimy liquid on the body of a new born infant.

Nalu (na'-lu), v. 1. To be in doubt or suspense; to suspend one's judgment. 2. To speak secretly, or to speak to one's self; to think within one's self. 3. To talk or confer together concerning a thing. 4. To think; to search after any truth or fact.

—from Lorrin Andrews' A Dictionary of
the Hawaiian Language, *Lahaina, Maui, 1865.*

Classical, semantical visions flash and sparkle to life in an introductory portfolio of photographs by some of surfing's finest camera artists. At right, local boy Larry Bertlemann contemplates sea and sky. Then, in sequence: Alec "Ace Cool" Cooke bails out at Waimea Bay (14–15); we experience a helicopter eye view of a lone Sunset surfer (16–17); top Hawaii professional Hans Hedemann high-performs at Oahu's Off-The-Wall (18); and Aussie Tom Carroll executes a splendid backside, off-the-lip maneuver in a Burleigh, Queensland shorebreak (19). See the Appendices section for a detailed listing of all photo and art credits.

Florida ace Matt Kechele slashes into an El Salvador beach break, below, while Ken Bradshaw, right, flies through a Pupukea blur.

Following pages: Inside Haleiwa and outside Avalanche frame the cool blue artistry of Hawaiian water man Buttons Kaluhiokalani.

Preceding pages: Jeffrey's Bay local Larry Levine races along an endless "Supertubes" wall generated by South Africa's Roaring 40's.

Warm California glimmers: left, at Huntington, and at little Rincon, right; meanwhile, in Maine, following pages, surfing in the snow.

LYRICAL POLYNESIAN ORIGINS

SURFING AS sensual physics. Surfing as rebirth. Surfing as a highly charged emotion. Surfing as a search for truth. Surfing as surfing.

He'enalu, the lyrical term adopted by ancient Hawaiian poets to describe their spectacular sport of surfing, is a word rich in nuance. Like many subtleties expressed by this highly-evolved and lately "discovered" civilization, the word for this popular form of recreation is rich in what Hawaiians call *kaona*, or hidden meanings.

Probably because they were a great seafaring culture, and also because they keenly studied and worshiped the animate and inanimate forces that created and surrounded their island nations, Polynesians attached great mystique to the ocean and her moods. Not unlike the Eskimo, who employs several hundred words to relate forms and concepts of ice and snow, the Polynesian likewise attributes numerous persona and poetic metaphors to the ever-changing sea, the *kai*.

She can be calm and quiet (*kai mālie*), in any of a dozen benign forms, or she can fume rough and raging (*kai pupule*). More sensuous allusions identify *streaked, whispering* and *silent* conditions. Sometimes she *swoons*. Puna, "the spring", she of "pouty lips", was a coastal region known for her "sea rustling over pebbles" (*Puna i ke kai nehe i ka 'ili'ili*). When she was smooth you could *punalua* — glide effortlessly, with a few paddles — into a wave. Even mellower is Kona, "the leeward wind," known for her "seas with cloud billows that forecast peace" (*Kona kai 'opua i kala i ka la'i*). A reasonable lady she.

All these natural forms, of course, had a significant effect on *he'enalu*, as any modern day surfer will readily testify. There was even a good Hawaiian word, *hōpūpū*, that referred to a state of being *stoked*, or emotionally excited, about something. In his important manuscript *Traditions of Hawaii*, the 19th Century Hawaiian scholar Kepelino Keauokalani (1830–1878), recalled that during November, which in the Hawaiian calendar is called *'Ikuwā*, in honor of "deafening" winds, storms and waves that occur during that month, early Hawaiians would become particularly *hōpūpū*.

'Ikuwā, wrote Kepelino, oftentimes entranced conscientious mortals and they would cast normal responsibilities aside.

It is a month of rough seas and high surf that lure men to the sea coast. For expert surfers going upland to farm, if part way up perhaps they look back and see the rollers combing the beach, will leave their work, pluck ripe banana leaves, ti leaves and ginger, strip them, fasten them about their necks and stand facing the sea and holding sugar-cane in their hand, then, hurrying away home, they will pick up the board and go. All thought of work is at an end, only that of sport is left. The wife may go hungry, the children, the whole family, but the head of the house does not care. He is all for sport, that is his food. All day there is nothing but surfing. Many go out surfing as early as four in the morning — men, women, children. There is fine sport; [then] from innocent pleasure they turn to evil pleasures; so it goes!

Stoked indeed. And if distant storms didn't generate suitable waves, surfers would enlist the aid of a *kahuna*, a sorcerer, and literally pray for surf. Abraham Fornander (1812–1887), a Maui Circuit Court judge who wrote *An Account of the Polynesian Race: Its Origins and Migrations*, collected an unusual chant used during ancient "surf coaxing rituals." This chant was called a *pōhuehue*, after the beach morning-glory (*Ipomoea pes-*

This charming surfing petroglyph was found by an archaeological team on a beach rock at Kona on the Big Island of Hawaii. He may or may not pre-date the "discovery" of Hawaii by non-Polynesians.

caprae), a hardy vine found on tropical beaches. If there was a serious dearth of surf in a particular area, the appointed *kahuna* would take several strands of the *pōhuehue* and, in unison with frustrated surfers, swing the vines around and lash them "unitedly upon the water until the desired undulating waves were obtained, at the same time chanting for a response to their efforts." The chant implored:

> *Inā 'a 'ohe nalu, a laila aku i kai, penei e hea ai:*
> (If there is no surf, invoke seaward in the following manner:)
> *Kū mai! Kū mai! Ka nalu nui mai Kahiki mai,*
> (Arise, arise you great surfs from Kahiki,)
> *Alo po 'i pū! Kū mai ka pōhuehue,*
> (The powerful curling waves. Arise with the *pōhuehue*.)
> *Hū! Kai ko 'o loa.*
> (Well up, long raging surf.)

John Francis Gray Stokes (1876–1960), in an archaeological study (*Ancient Worship of the Hawaii Islanders*) compiled by William T. Brigham, the first director of Hawaii's Bernice Pauahi Bishop Museum, wrote in 1919 of a seaside *heiau* (temple) at Kahaluu Bay on the Kona coast where Hawaiian natives made offerings and prayed to their gods for good surfing conditions. That *heiau*, called Ku'emanu, was identified by local Hawaiians as "a *heiau* for surf-riders, where they could pray for good sport." Stokes observed that there was a bleachers-like terrace where spectators could watch surfers in action, and within the temple compound's confines was a brackish pool where surfers could rinse away saltwater after a waveriding session.

Sometimes, according to another Fornander-translated legend, a demigod would intercede in surfers' behalf. A chant about Laenihi, a Hawaiian woman with celebrated mystical powers, recalls how she forced winds to blow and caused "the sea to be aroused from its calm repose." This wave-generating wind, called the *Unulau* (or trade wind), did its mystical thing, and, as the chant notes: "Early that morning the surf began to roll in. When the people rose from their sleep and saw the surf, they all began to shout and yell." Within moments they had grabbed their boards and paddled out to "where the rollers began to curve up."

Because the Polynesians never developed a "printed language" per se, they were highly evolved as a "chanting culture." Stories such as the above were committed to memory and from generation to generation. In other words, they communicated their news, histories and commentaries about day-to-day life by means of spoken songs or chants, called *mele*. Until early Westerners, primarily Christian missionaries, arrived, alphabetized their language and impressed "printed words" into their culture, the Polynesians had to rely on these oral histories for virtually all known intelligence about their living culture and ancestral traditions.

Some scholars contend that the sounds and movements of the sea established the sounds, movements and rhythms of the earliest chants and dances of Polynesia. Even in modern Hawaii, notes theologian John Charlot, "students of chanting practice on the beach to reproduce the modulations of waves." Winona Beamer, a contemporary *kumu hula*, or teacher of *hula*, recalled during a recent interview with Honolulu author Jerry Hopkins that her grandmother, Helen Desha Beamer, taught ancient Hawaiian chant and dance forms by taking her and fellow students to the beach and instructing them to "observe the rise and fall of the surf and to get into it and mimic the ebb and surge."

This tandem surfer was incised by ancient Hawaiians on a lava rock found in a petroglyph field above Kaunolū Bay on the "spirit island" of Lanai. It was at Kaunolū that Kamehameha the Great maintained a favorite summer home.

This fine, hand-colored engraving of Hawaiian domestic life was rendered by the French artist Jacques Arago. It portrays the helmeted chief Kalanimoku, a kapa-beating wife, and a fine study of an 'olo surfboard: From the voyage of the corvette Uranie, 1817-1820. Engraving by Andrew Pellion.

"She had us stand on top of huge boulders by the ocean and practice chanting over the sound of the waves. The sea breeze, sometimes a wind, rushed in. The surf, turning paisley where it rolled in over the reef, bounded in pure energy toward us. As the waves grew and came nearer we stood firmly and chanted louder, louder—until the waves broke in fantastic turquoise and white plumes. Even as we got doused, we chanted. And as the water ran back to the sea, we chanted more softly. Often our names were the chant.

"Sometimes a wave would curl on the beach, then make delicate ripples before it slipped back into the depths. As it moved away, we were supposed to hold a quavering trill until another set of waves started toward us . . ."

Known chants that have to do with surfing—or surfing's physical and metaphysical effect(s) on mind and body—are too numerous to recount here, but those that are mentioned illustrate the role surfing played in the social and spiritual lives of ancient Polynesian practitioners. Thomas G. Thrum's *Hawaiian Annual* for the year 1896 notes that "Surf riding was one of the favorite Hawaiian sports, in which chiefs, men, women and youth took a lively interest. Much valuable time was spent by them in this practice throughout the day."

The Thrum article emphasizes that the sport had such a hold on its devotees that "necessary work for the maintenance of the family . . . was often neglected for the prosecution of the sport." The sport, however, was not attractive only for aesthetic and recreational reasons. It was also a big betting game, one on which the Hawaiians of old would wager their most important properties. "Canoes, nets, fishing lines, kapas, swine, poultry and all other property were staked," Thrum's recalls, "and in some instances life itself was put up as wagers, the property changing hands, and personal liberty, or even life itself, sacrificed according to the outcome of the match, the winners carrying off their riches and the losers and their families passing to a life of poverty or servitude."

The most common scholarly question about surfing has to do with its origins. Nobody can quite pin down just where this dance form was born. Who first meditated on the use of gravity and moving wave vectors? And who shaped the first surfboard and paddled into that first wave?

Origin theories rise and crash. Tom Blake, that fast-swimming native of Wisconsin who immigrated to Hawaii and California and did so much to "modernize" surfing, believes in a theory that surfing was developed not in Polynesia, but in Equatorial West Africa. He once cited a report by a traveler, Alexander, who observed surfing in that part of the Black Continent in 1837. Most surfing anthropologists defer to the sighting of surfing by the British Captain James Cook, who in 1777 observed canoe and body surfing in the Society Islands, and later, in 1778, marveled at the sight of board surfing in the Sandwich Isles (Hawaii). Meanwhile, contemporary surf historian Ben Finney, in his *Surfboarding in Oceania: its Pre-European Distribution*, notes that "an extensive examination of the available sources has shown that surfboarding was known in Polynesia, Micronesia, and Melanesia. In fact, surfboarding was practiced in Oceania from New Guinea in the West, to Easter Island in the East, and from Hawaii in the North to New Zealand in the South."

Finney cites sightings of various forms of primitive surfing in places as diverse as Owa Raha in the Solomon Islands (observed, 1949) to Yap in the Western Carolines (observed by a colleague) and even as far south as the New Hebrides and Fiji. "With reservations," he asserts, this "wide distribution would seem to indicate that surfboarding is a general Oceanic sport, rather than a specifically Polynesian sport." Whatever its origins or

[*Frontispiece.*

"Kahéle and I watched the surf-swimmers for some time, charmed with the spectacle."—(*See p.* 234.)

distribution, however, Finney agrees that its greatest renown "can be traced to Polynesian influence," and in particular that of Hawaiian Polynesia. More detailed incidents of its "discovery" by outsiders follow.

Surfing myths have been collected in remote Polynesian places such as Samoa, Tahiti and New Zealand, but by far the greatest number of surfing legends have been documented in Hawaii. Then, as now, Hawaiian surf stories were *da best*. They sang of mystical spirit guardians, petty jealousies, physical prowess and tenacious lust.

Consider the following dragon myth recounted by the Hawaiian journalist Samuel Manaiakalani Kamakau (1815–1876):

Kalamainu'u lived at Makaleha in the Waialua district on Oahu. She had a cave on the west side of Wailea Valley. She was really a *mo'o*, a "serpent," with a long, detachable tongue, which she later gave to her husband to use as a surfboard. He was Puna'ai-koa'e, a descendant of chiefs of Kauai, who lived at Kapa'a in Puna. A skilled surfer, he was out one day surfing. He saw a beautiful woman on a long board and jumped on it to make love to her. By her power she drew him out to sea and then around to shore near her home. The two went to the woman's Wailea cave, where for several months they remained making love until the young man lost his good looks and yearned for the waves of his native land. He told his wife, "sitting with her bright hair streaming, reddened and shining," that he wanted to go surfing...

Early surfing scenes were also fanciful, fun, bitchy and, oftentimes, violent. Gourmets might savor accounts of a post-surfing *lū'au*, where the menu consisted of chicken wings boiled in blood, vegetarian-fed "poi dogs" roasted in an *imu* (underground oven) and draughts of 'awa (*Piper methysticum*), that numbing intoxicant long favored and drunk by Polynesians. Soap opera fans, meanwhile, would appreciate the complexity of ancient Hawaiian surfside romances. They would weep at the story of the handsome man, Kiha-a-Pii-lani, and his lover, Kolea-moku, who despite a strict *kapu* eloped and lived a life of *aloha* opposite their favorite surf spot. In deference to "evil pleasures," as the latter-day Christian Kepelino called such sexual encounters, let's look in on this ancient love affair at Hana on the island of Maui. As our narrator, Kamakau, tells the story:

... Kiha-a-Pii-lani had a perfect physique and was good-looking from head to feet, without mark or blemish. Because he lived in comfort and ate properly, his body filled out. His constant bathing in the sea reddened his cheeks to the color of a cooked crab, and [made] his eyes as bright as those of a *moho'ea* bird. The surf on which Ho'olae's daughter [Kolea-moku] surfed was Keanini. It was inside the bay of Kapueokahi, a surf that broke easily. Ho'olae's daughter was accustomed to surf-riding. Kiha-a-Pii-lani was used to surfing at Waikiki, and he often boasted of those with a long sweep, the surf of Ka-lehua-wehe and the surf of Mai-hiwa. Two to four days Kiha-a-Pii-lani and Kolea-moku spent in surf-riding. Noticing his handsome appearance Kolea-moku made love to him. The girl was determined to have him for a husband but her father was set against it because she was betrothed to the ruling chief, Lono-a-Piilani. The flowers wilted in the sunlight [however] when she saw this other man...

The fanciful, dreamlike apparition at left appeared as the frontispiece in Charles William Stoddard's rococo travel volume titled Summer Cruising in the South Seas, 1874. *The illustrator was Wallis Mackay. "Such buoyancy of material matter I had never dreamed of," said Stoddard. "Across the level water, heads, hands, and shoulders, and sometimes half-bodies, were floating about, like the* amphibia."

The seductive, bare-breasted surf maiden at right appeared in an exotic 19th Century guide to the Sandwich Isles. She brings to mind a line from the early Christian missionary Hiram Bingham, who noted upon his arrival that, "As we proceeded to the shore, the multitudinous, shouting and almost naked savages, of every age, sex, and rank, swimming, floating on surf-boards, sailing in canoes, attracted our earnest attention."

Surfing as courtship is further corroborated in an important surfing story published in the December 23, 1865 issue of *Nupepa Kuokoa*, one of Honolulu's early Hawaiian language newspapers. In an article about *Ancient Sports of Hawaii (Ka Holomana Kahiko)* the Hawaiian journalist J. Waimau recalls that at periodic surfing contests held in old Hawaii, the men, looking like "a company of soldiers of that day," would wear red-dyed *malo* (loincloths) and assemble on the beach. Women, he wrote, would appear on the beach in matching red-dyed *kapa* skirts, and "they [would] go and join together with the men in surfriding. In their surfing, a man and a woman will ride in on the same surf. Such riding in of the man and woman on the same surf is termed vanity, and results in sexual indulgence."

One of Hawaii's most recounted surfing epics dates to the time of the great Hawaiian chief Umi, who ruled over the entirety of the Big Island of Hawaii and Maui during the late 15th and early 16th centuries. Kamakau writes that when Umi was a young man he was renowned as a surfrider. One day "a certain chief of Laupahoehoe noticed Umi's skill in surfriding."

His name was Paiea, and he knew all the surfs and the best one to ride. It was the one directly in front of Laupahoehoe, facing Hilo. It was a huge one which none dared to ride except Paiea, who was noted for his skill. Gambling on surfing was practiced in that locality. All of the inhabitants from Waipunalei to Kaula placed their wager on Umi, and those of Laupahoehoe on Paiea. The two rode the surf, and while surfing Paiea noticed that Umi was winning. As they drew near a rock, Paiea crowded him against it, skinning his side. Umi was strong and pressed his foot against Paiea's chest and then landed ashore. Umi won against Paiea, and because he crowded Umi against the rock with the intention of killing him, Paiea was roasted in an *imu* [an oven] [in later years when Umi became the supreme king of the Big Island].

Even more spectacular is a Kamakau surfing yarn that documents a surfing dogfight between a rebel surfer and a giant shark. This story is recounted in Chapter IX ("Events of Kal-lani-'opuu's Time") of Kamakau's Hawaiian source book, *Ruling Chiefs of Hawaii*. It tells of negative energy kahuna priests, a power-hungry chief, Ka-lani-'opuu, and the surfer-revolutionary, Nuuanupahu, who was a popular chief in the Big Island's Ka'u District. The brave chief Nuuanupahu is ultimately killed by the huge shark, but his surfing and fighting bravery has been immortalized in one of Hawaii's most exciting royalty myths.

Probably because surfing was heartily endorsed by the chiefly class (the *ali'i*) as well as the working class (the *maka'ainana*), it achieved a special status and respectability in ancient Hawaii. Renowned surfers were celebrated in song and dance and often enjoyed special privileges in royal circles. In his *Polynesian Researches*, the Christian missionary William Ellis (1794–1872) recalls that Kaumualii, the great *mō'i* (king) from the island of Kauai, was renowned as an accomplished surfer. Ellis also recalls seeing the elderly Big Island chiefs Karaimoku and Kakioena, "both between fifty and sixty years of age, and large corpulent men, balancing themselves on their long and narrow boards, or splashing about in the foam, with as much satisfaction as youths of sixteen."

Though a territorial or greedy chief could *kapu* (make off limits) a favorable surfing spot for the private use of himself and his best friends, surfing, contrary to some myths, was a sport en-

SURF BATHING

Drawn by F.A. Olmsted.

Lith of Endicott. N.Y.

SANDWICH ISLANDERS PLAYING IN THE SURF

joyed by all Hawaiians, whatever their caste. Personal wealth, however, often dictated the quality of waveriding gear. A chief, for example, could order a team of retainers to trek into the cold highlands and cut down a favorite *koa* or *wiliwili* tree for his board. The finest craftsmen in his *ahupua'a* (or ruling realm) would then carefully custom-shape his *papa he'enalu* with adzes. Poorer commoners had to make do with simpler wave-riding vehicles. The Hawaiian chronicler John Papa Ii (1800–1870) recalls, in a description of surfing at Lahaina, Maui in 1812, that "boys were surfing on the north side of Pelekane, with banana trunks for surfboards . . ."

However humble one's surfboard, it was treated with respect. Even before the board was shaped, according to the 1896 *Thrum's*, a proper "surfbuilding ritual" was observed:

> The uninitiated were naturally careless, or indifferent to the method of cutting the chosen tree; but among those who desired success upon their labors the following rites were carefully observed:
> Upon the selection of a suitable tree, a red fish called *kumu* was first procured, which was placed at its trunk. The tree was then cut down, after which a hole was dug at its root and the fish placed therein, with a prayer, as an offering in payment therefor. After the ceremony was performed, then the tree trunk was chipped away from each side until reduced to a board approximately of the dimensions desired, when it was pulled down to the beach and placed in the *halau* (canoe house) or other such suitable place convenient for the finishing work.

In one of Hawaiiana's most interesting commentaries on early surfing equipment, the scholar Ii explains that there were three types of Hawaiian surfboards commonly in use — the *'olo*, the *kiko'o* and the *alaia*.

"The *'olo* is thick in the middle and grows thinner toward the edges. It is a good board for a wave that swells and rushes shoreward but not for a wave that rises up high and curls over. If it is not moved sideways when the wave rises high, it is tossed upward as it moves shoreward.

"The *kiko'o* reaches a length of 12 to 18 feet and is good for a surf that breaks roughly. This board is good for surfing, but it is hard to handle. Other surfers are afraid of it because of its length and its great speed on a high wave that is about to curl over. It can ride on all the risings of the wave in its way until they subside and the board reaches shore.

"The *alaia* board, which is 9 feet long, is thin and wide in front, tapering toward the back. On a rough wave, this board vibrates against the rider's abdomen, chest, or hands when they rest flat on it, or when the fingers are gripped into a fist at the time of landing. Because it tends to go downward and cut through a wave it does not rise up with the wave as it begins to curl over. Going into a wave is one way to stop its gliding, and going onto the curl is another. Skilled surfers use it frequently, but the unskilled are afraid of this board, choosing rather to sit on a canoe or to surf on even smaller boards."

There is not a great deal of information available in Hawaiian language literature about the construction and maintenance of surfboards, but reports by early foreigners indicate that a person's surfboard was considered a special property. The missionary Ellis observed in 1822 that Hawaiian surfboards were stained black, and following a surfing session were carefully dried, rubbed over with coconut oil, then "frequently wrapped in cloth and suspended in some part of their house."

The adventurer-writer Francis Allyn Olmsted (Incidents of a Whaling Voyage, 1841) was also a pretty good sketch artist— as one can see in his whimsical picture, left, of "Sandwich Islanders Playing in the Surf." Olmsted recalled that Hawaii's waveriding natives "dashed impetuously towards the shore, guiding themselves with admirable skill and apparent unconsciousness of danger . . ."

And in 1825 the British Captain George Anson Byron, master of *HMS Blonde* (and a cousin to the poet Lord George Gordon Byron), recorded in his ship's log that "to have a neat floatboard, well-kept, and dried, is to a Sandwich Islander what a tilbury or cabriolet, or whatever light carriage may be in fashion is to a young English man."

In a commentary on the "Finishing Process" involved in producing a surfboard, the aforementioned and unknown *Thrum's* authors offer the following shaping room intelligence:

> Coral of the corrugated variety termed *pohauku puna*, which could be gathered in abundance along the sea beach, and a rough kind of stone called *oahi*, were the commonly used articles for reducing and smoothing the rough surfaces of the board until all marks of the stone adze [used to shape the board from a tree trunk] were obliterated. As a finishing stain the root of the ti plant (*Cordyline terminalis*), called *mole ki*, or the pounded bark of the *kukui* (*Aleurites moluccana*), called *hili*, was the mordant used for a paint made with the root of burned kukui nuts. This furnished a durable, glossy black finish, far preferable to that made with the ashes of burned cane leaves, or amau fern, which had neither body nor gloss.

Some ancient Hawaiian surfboards are kept in private homes and in the collection of Honolulu's Bernice Pauahi Bishop Museum, but probably the oldest *known* board is a small "floater" that belonged to a much-beloved Big Island chiefess who enjoyed surfing during the early to mid-1600s.

This rare surfboard is described in a charming story published in the December 8, 1905 issue of the *Hawaiian Gazette*, a then popular semi-weekly Honolulu newspaper. According to a page 6 dispatch headlined "Sled of a Chiefess," N. K. Pukui, while on a tour of the island of Hawaii (as a traveling agent of the Hawaiian Realty and Maturity Co.) found an ancient sled and surfboard in a burial cave at Hoʻokena:

> It is said that the oldest *kamaainas* of Hookena have heard from their parents and grandparents that sometime in the reign of King Keawenuiaumi, about two hundred and fifty or three hundred years ago, a high chiefess named Kaneamuna was then living at Hookena. Her principal amusement was *hee holua* (coasting on a sled) and *hee nalu* (surfing).
> She had her people make a sliding ground for her on a hill just back of the little village of Hookena, and ordered a sled, or land toboggan, called a *papa holua*, as well as a surfing board, or a *papa hee nalu*. When the slide was finished she passed many pleasant hours sliding down the steep hill. This slide was composed of smooth stones covered with rushes. After her death her sled and surf board disappeared, and the secret of their hiding-place was never revealed. It is believed the sled and board found in the cave belonged to the High Chiefess. They are made of the wood of the bread-fruit tree (the *ʻulu*) and at the present time are in very good condition . . .

Even the most renowned and powerful chiefess in Hawaiian history — Kaahumanu, the Queen Regent and favorite wife of Kamehameha the Great — was an enthusiastic surfer. Indeed, Kamehameha and Kaahumanu were probably the most celebrated couple in surfing history. Kamehameha (1753?–1819) and Kaahumanu (1768–1832), according to author Ii (in Chapter X, "Life in Kona," of his *Fragments of Hawaiian History*), were particularly fond of surfing at Kooka, a wave spot located at Pua'a in North Kona "where a coral head stands just outside a point of lava rocks. Or as Ii remembers:

> When the surf dashed over the coral head, the people swam out with their surfboards and floated with them. If a person owned a long narrow canoe, he performed what was called *lele wa'a*, or canoe leaping, in which the surfer leaped off the canoe with his board and rode the crest of a wave ashore. The canoe slid back of the wave because of the force of the shove given it with the feet. When the surfer drew close to the place where the surf rose, a wave would pull itself up high and roll in. Any timid person who got too close to it was overwhelmed and could not reach the landing place. The opening through which the surfer entered was like a sea pool, with a rocky hill above and rows of lava rocks on both sides, and deep in the center. This was a difficult feat and not often seen, but for Kaahumanu and the King [Kamehameha] it was easy. When they reached the place where the surf rose high, they went along with the crest of a wave and slipped into the sea pool before the wave rolled over. Only the light spray of the surf touched them before they reached the pool. The spectators shouted and remarked to each other how clever the two were . . .

And so *he'enalu* flowed on, and like ancient dolphins at play in a remote part of the world, the isolated Hawaiians kept this water sport magic to themselves for several centuries. They, and only they, knew the wonder of being borne so swiftly by the unpredictable sea. Only they stood up and played with large vibrations of water pumped their way by wild storms in the frozen north and south. Only they. Until one day late in the 18th Century a strange thing happened: Unusual "floating islands," massive watercraft with white billowing wings, appeared on their horizons. As Kamakau described this apparition:

> Chiefs and commoners saw the wonderful sight and marveled at it. Some were terrified and shrieked with fear. The valley of Waimea rang with the shouts of the excited people as they saw the boat with its masts and sails shaped like a gigantic sting ray. One asked another, "What are those branching things?" and the other answered, "They are trees moving on the sea." Still another thought, "A double canoe of the hairless ones of Mana!" A certain kahuna named Kuohu declared, "That can be nothing else than the heiau of Lono, the tower of Keolewa, and the place of sacrifice at the altar." The excitement became more intense, and louder grew the shouting.

Upon seeing these terrifying things, the Hawaiians first fled, went into hiding, and prayed in fright. Then, becoming bolder, they began venturing closer to their shores, and braver ones began waving *aloha* to these visiting gods. Eventually, after fearful inhibitions had been discarded, the Hawaiians took to the water and slowly paddled out to sea — in outrigger canoes and on surfboards — to marvel at these fair-skinned deities at close range.

It was under such awesome and historical circumstances, bobbing in offshore waters, that the white man, the *haole*, met his first surfer.

J. Webber del.

A View of KARAKA

W. Byrne sculp.

OA, in OWYHEE.

'A MOST SUPREME PLEASURE'

THE WESTERN world got its first look at the apparition variously described as "surf bathing," "surf playing" and "dancing among the combers" in the journals of sea captains, missionaries, adventurers and traveling journalists of the 18th and 19th centuries. Visual impressions were rare, but a number of fine, albeit fanciful, surfing studies, most of them by adventurous European ships' artists, have survived.

These descriptions and visions of "Sandwich Isle natives at play in the surf" were well received in England, America and on the Continent. Understandably so. After all, where else on Earth had a culture devised a recreation so subtle — yet at the same time so spectacular — as *he'enalu*?

Appropriately, the first surfing report filed by a Westerner was one sensitively penned by the British explorer, Captain James Cook, he who often is identified as "the greatest navigator the world has ever known."

Cook and his colleagues didn't witness actual stand-up board surfing until they "discovered" Hawaii in 1778, but about a year earlier, in December of 1777, they observed the wonders of canoe surfing while at anchorage at Tahiti's Matavai Point. In an essay that is Cook at his literary best, the insightful Captain commented on the therapeutic and aesthetic natures of surfing. Or as he explains:

> Neither are they [the Tahitians] strangers to the soothing effects produced by particular sorts of motion, which in some cases seem to allay any perturbation of mind with as much success as music. Of this I met with a remarkable instance. For on walking one day about Matavai Point, where our tents were erected, I saw a man paddling in a small canoe so quickly, and looking about him with such eagerness on each side, as to command my attention. At first I imagined that he had stolen something from one of the ships, and was pursued; but, on waiting patiently, saw him repeat his amusement. He went out from the shore till he was near the place where the swell begins to take its rise; and, watching its first motion very attentively, paddled before it with great quickness, till he found that it overlooked him, and had acquired sufficient force to carry his canoe before it without passing underneath. He then sat motionless, and was carried along at the same swift rate as the wave, till it landed him upon the beach. Then he started out, emptied his canoe, and went in search of another swell. I could not help concluding that this man felt the most supreme pleasure while he was driven on so fast and so smoothly by the sea; especially as, though the tents and ships were so near, he did not seem in the least to envy or even to take any notice of the crowds of his countrymen collected to view them as objects which were rare and curious. During my stay, two or three of the natives came up, who seemed to share his felicity, and always called out when there was an appearance of a favourable swell, as he sometimes missed it by his back being turned, and looking about for it. By then I understood that this exercise, which is called "choroee," was frequent amongst them; and they have probably more amusements of this sort which afford them at least as much pleasure as skating, which is the only of ours with whose effects I could compare it.

> — from Volume 11,
> Chapter IX of
> *Cook's Voyages*

The detailed bayscape on the preceding pages documents the January 17, 1779 arrival of Captain James Cook at Kealakekua, Hawaii. In the foreground is the first known Western image of a surfer on his board. At left, that image in larger detail. This Cook voyage engraving was based on an original study by the artist to the expedition, John Webber.

Cook's detailed account of surfing corroborates what all surfers know: Surfing, then and now, has a near hypnotic effect, and if the waves are good, nothing — not even the appearance of exotic foreigners — will distract a surfer from his sport. Cook, a lifelong mariner who had great love and respect for the sea, well understood such preoccupation.

Perhaps a thousand years before Cook visited Tahiti, Tahitians, and neighboring Marquesans, had sailed north in the Pacific to Hawaii, a land identified in ancient Polynesian chants as *Hawai'ia*, or "Burning Hawaii" (probably in reference to her active volcanoes). To the isolated Hawaiian archipelago these migrant Tahitians and Marquesans carried common cultural traits, foods, ancient oral traditions and, of course, favorite forms of recreation, including *he'enalu*. It was in and about Hawaii's more benevolent reefs, beaches and headland points that the *haole*, beginning with Cook and company, observed surfing in its most highly developed state.

Cook probably would have filed an excellent Hawaiian surfing dispatch, but both his navigating and writing careers were ended abruptly on February 14, 1779, when a group of angry Hawaiians attacked and killed him and four of his marines in the shallows of Kealakekua Bay on the Big Island's Kona Coast. However, Cook's Lieutenant, James King, recounted the spectacle that was surfing in 18th Century Hawaii.

King notes (in Volume III of *A Voyage to the Pacific Ocean*) that in Hawaii "swimming is not only a necessary art, in which their men and women are more expert than any people we had hitherto seen, but a favorite diversion among them." Of surfing, an "exercise" which "appeared to us most perilous and extraordinary," King wrote: "The boldness and address, with which we saw them perform these difficult and dangerous maneuvres was altogether astonishing, and is scarcely to be credited."

As evidence of his astonishment, King devoted nearly two full pages of book text to descriptions of surfing techniques, preferred wave conditions, and variable surfing styles he observed at Karakakooa [now spelled Kealakekua] Bay. "The surf, which breaks on the coast round the bay," he noted, "extends to the distance of about one hundred and fifty yards from the shore, within which space, the surges of the sea, accumulating from the shallowness of the water, are dashed against the beach with prodigious violence. Whenever, from stormy weather, or any extraordinary swell at sea, the impetuosity of the surf is increased to its utmost height, they [the Hawaiians] choose that time for this amusement . . .'"

King said that wipeouts in rocky areas were "reckoned very disgraceful" and were "attended with the loss of the board, which I have often seen, with great terror, dashed to pieces, at the very moment the islander quitted it."

Unfortunately, no formal drawings of surfing were rendered by the Cook voyage's official artist, John Webber. However, in one of his most famous scenic studies, titled "A View of Karakakooa, in Owyhee," a lone surfer is seen in the foreground, paddling a blunt-nosed surfboard alongside a group of outrigger canoes that are heading seaward to greet the British ships *Resolution* and *Discovery*. Except for recently discovered petroglyphs which may or may not pre-date Cook's arrival, this Webber study is the first known illustration of a surfboard.

Following the publication of Cook's and King's logs in widely circulated volumes sponsored by the Lords Commissioners of the British Admiralty, Hawaii became *the* exotic Mid-Pacific destination on many a curious sea captain's itinerary. And consequently, during the next century of

The oil painting at left was painted by an unknown artist who visited Hawaii about 1850. It is painted on a biscuit tin and is titled: "Hawaiian Surfing, ca. 1850, at Hilo Bay, Hawaii." The work was recently discovered in a New York art gallery by a Honolulu antiquarian who has since returned it to Honolulu.

49

Cover, below, from a travel volume by Charles Warren Stoddard, 1874.

exploration and discovery, more people learned about the Hawaiian and his surfboard. Oftentimes that was a visitor's very first impression, long before he or she made a proper landing on shore.

Archibald Campbell, in his *A Voyage Round the World, from 1806 to 1812*, remembered that "from their earliest years, the natives [of Hawaii] spend much of their spare time in the water, and constant practice renders them so dexterous, that they seem as much at their ease in that element as on land; they often swim several miles off to ships, sometimes resting upon a plank shaped like an anchor stock, and paddling with their hands, but more frequently without any assistance whatever."

A dozen or so years later, the author-missionary Ellis (in his 1826 *Narrative of a Tour Through Hawaii*) observed that "the fondness of the natives for the water must strike any person visiting their islands; long before he goes on shore, he will see them swimming around his ship; and few ships leave without being accompanied part of the way out of the harbour by the natives, sporting in the water; but to see fifty or a hundred persons riding on an immense billow, half immersed in spray and foam, for a distance of several hundred yards together, is one of the most novel and interesting sports a foreigner can witness in the islands."

Another missionary was so taken by surfing that he wrote: "Many a man from abroad who has witnessed this exhilarating play, has no doubt only wished that he were free and able to share in it himself. For my part, I should like nothing better, if I could do it, than to get balanced on a board just before a great rushing wave, and so be hurried in half or quarter of a mile landward with the speed of a race-horse, all the time enveloped in foam and spray, but without letting the roller break and tumble over my head."

That author with the adventurous soul was the Reverend Henry T. Cheever, writing in his book *Life in the Sandwich Islands, The Heart of the Pacific, As It Was and Is* (1851). He made his comments after observing surfing in the Lahaina area on the island of Maui.

"It is highly amusing to a stranger," he wrote, "to go out into the south part of this town, some day when the sea is rolling in heavily over the reef, and to observe there the evolutions and rapid career of a company of surf-players." Cheever noted that the sport of surfing "is so attractive and full of wild excitement to Hawaiians, and withal so healthy, that I cannot but hope it will be many years before civilization shall look it out of countenance, or make it disreputable to indulge in this manly, though it be dangerous, exercise."

Cheever points out that surfing requires "strength of muscle and sleight-of-hand, to keep the head and shoulders just ahead and clear of the great crested wall that is every moment impending over one, and threatening to bury the bold surf-rider in its wary ruin," but he also emphasized that it was a sport for all sexes and ages.

"Even the huge Premier (Ahuea) has been known to commit her bulky person to a surfboard; and the chiefs generally, when they visit Lahaina, take a turn or two at this invigorating sport with billows and board."

Ten years earlier, another adventurer, Francis Allyn Olmsted, author of *Incidents of a Whaling Voyage* (1841), in a commentary on Hawaiian "Aquatic Feats," recalled his first impressions of surfing, which he witnessed at Kailua-Kona in July, 1840.

After taking a stroll "down to the sea shore, where a party of natives were playing in the surf, which was thundering upon the beach," Olmsted wrote:

Each of them had a *surf board*, a smooth flat board from six to eight feet long, by twelve

---

526 NATIVE SURF BATHING.

beastly porpoises engaged at their eternal game of arching over a wave and disappearing, and then doing it over again and keeping it up—always circling over, in that way, like so many well-submerged wheels. But the porpoises wheeled themselves away, and then we were thrown upon our own resources. It did not take many minutes to discover that the sun was blazing like a bonfire, and that the weather was of a melting temperature. It had a drowsing effect, too.

In one place we came upon a large company of naked natives, of both sexes and all ages, amusing themselves with the national pastime of surf-bathing. Each heathen would paddle three or four hundred yards out to sea, (taking a short board with him), then face the shore and wait for a particularly prodigious billow to come along; at the right moment he would fling his board upon its foamy crest and himself upon the board, and here he would come whizzing by like a bombshell! It did not seem that a lightning express train could shoot along at a more hair-lifting speed. I tried surf-bathing once, subsequently, but made a failure of it. I got the board placed right, and at the right moment, too; but missed the connection myself.—The board struck the shore in three quarters of a second, without any cargo, and I struck the bottom about the same time, with a couple of barrels of water in me. None but natives ever master the art of surf-bathing thoroughly.

At the end of an hour, we had made the four miles, and landed on a level point of land, upon which was a wide extent of old ruins, with many a tall cocoanut tree growing among them. Here was the ancient City of Refuge—a vast inclosure, whose stone walls were twenty feet thick at the base,

SURF-BATHING—FAILURE.

A romantic French artist, E. Riou, titled the wispy female surfing scene at right "Jeux Haviens." This engraving, with a Tahiti-like backdrop, appeared in a popular 1873 travel anthology titled Qatorze Ans Aux Iles Sandwich.

to fifteen inches broad. Upon these, they plunged forward into the surf, diving under a roller as it broke in foam over them, until they arrived where the rollers were formed, a quarter of a mile from shore perhaps, when watching a favorable opportunity, they rose upon some huge breaker, and balancing themselves, either by kneeling upon their boards or extending themselves full length, they dashed impetuously towards the shore, guiding themselves with admirable skill and apparent unconsciousness of danger, in their lightning-like courses, while the bursting combers broke upon each side of them, with a deafening noise. In this way, they amuse themselves hour after hour, in sports which have too terrific an aspect for a foreigner to attempt, but which are admirably adapted to the almost amphibious character of the natives.

During the 1860s, several intrepid authors arrived in Hawaii and found themselves entranced by surfing. Even Mark Twain could not resist the siren call of the surf. In Chapter XXXII of his 1866 book, *Roughing It*, Twain writes of his first and last surfing experience:

I tried surf-bathing once, subsequently, but made a failure of it. I got the board placed right, and at the right moment, too; but missed the connection myself. The board struck the shore in three-quarters of a second, without any cargo, and I struck the bottom about the same time, with a couple of barrels of water in me.

Twain's adventure took place during a tour of the Kona Coast on the Big Island of Hawaii. He described the setting and circumstance:

In one place we came upon a large company of naked natives, of both sexes and all ages, amusing themselves with the national pastime of surf-bathing. Each heathen would paddle three or four hundred yards out to sea (taking a short board with him), then face the shore and wait for a particularly prodigious billow to come along; at the right moment he would fling his board upon its foamy crest and himself upon the board, and here he would come whizzing by like a bombshell! It did not seem that a lightning express train could shoot along at a more hair-lifting speed.

The celebrated adventurer-author Isabella L. Bird Bishop, wrote in 1874 that she "thoroughly enjoyed" an afternoon she spent watching surf-bathing at Hilo Bay. "It [surfing] is really a most exciting pastime, and in a rough sea requires immense nerve," she recalled in her 1875 book titled *The Hawaiian Archipelago, Six Months Among the Palm Groves, Coral Reefs, & Volcanoes of the Sandwich Islands.*

Mrs. Bishop described the surfboards being used at Hilo as "a tough plank shaped like a coffin lid, about two feet broad, and from six to nine feet long, well oiled and cared for. It is usually made of the erythrina, or the breadfruit tree." After paddling out to sea, she said, the many surfers in the water "re-appeared as a number of black heads bobbing about like corks in smooth water half a mile from shore." And after successfully paddling into a wave, "they rode in majestically, always just ahead of the breaker, carried shorewards by its mighty impulse at the rate of forty miles an hour, yet seeming to have a volition of their own . . ."

One would assume by these reports that the sport of surfing was in a splendid state of affairs. However, the opposite was true. Surfing, not un-

The loinclothed Waikiki local at right displays a small alaia surfboard that pre-dates the so-called "short board revolution" by some 80 years. This fine surfer study, ca. 1900, was shot by Honolulu photographer Frank Davey. On the following pages are two more short-boarders, ca. 1900, but this time at well-waved Hilo Bay, on the Big Island of Hawaii.

like nearly every other aspect of Hawaiian cultural life, was in a sad state of decline.

This decline is usually attributed to two culture shock factors, the first being the near destruction of the Hawaiian race by foreign disease. During their first century of exposure to the West, the long isolated, and thus genetically weaker, Hawaiian race shrank from an estimated population of 300,000 at the time of Captain Cook's first visit in 1778 to about 40,000 by 1893. This alone explains why surf spots had become less frequented.

The second reason for surfing's decline had to do with "the introduction of letters" — that is, education — by zealous missionaries and other non-Hawaiian educators. Indeed, how can anyone imbued with a Puritan education and work ethic justify the time needed to master such a complicated, and some would say frivolous, pastime? The straight-laced religionists prevalent in Hawaii during the 19th Century frowned upon surfing's seminudity and sexual connotations. They also deplored the drinking and gambling that often took place at competitive surfing contests. Thus, such "immoralities" were sternly discouraged.

An archaeologist, writing in a collection of 19th Century *Hawaiian Ethnological Notes* on file in Honolulu's Bernice Pauahi Bishop Museum, says, "It [surfing] was one of the famous sports of the olden times, but after the introduction of letters its popularity began to decline, simply because the people became more interested in the new learning introduced by their white teachers, not because of any opposition to the sport by the missionaries."

Hiram Bingham, leader of the first party of 14 Calvinist missionaries to arrive in 1820 in Hawaii, wrote in 1847: "The decline and discontinuance of the use of the surfboard, as civilization advances, may be accounted for by the increase in modesty, industry or religion, without supposing, as some have affected to believe, that missionaries caused oppressive enactments against it." This was the same Bingham who, upon arriving in Hawaii, wrote from shipside: "The appearance of destitution, degradation, and barbarism, among the chattering, and almost naked savages, whose heads and feet, and much of their sunburnt skins were bare, was appalling. Some of our number, with gushing tears, turned away from the spectacle. Others, with firmer nerve, continued their gaze, but were ready to exclaim, 'Can these be human beings?! . . . Can such things be civilized?'" He no doubt was describing a covey of laughing surfers — men, women and children — who had paddled out to meet the missionary ship *Thaddeus*.

In 1892, a year before the overthrow of the Hawaiian monarchy, Nathaniel B. Emerson, an author/anthropologist who took particular interest in "disappearing" Hawaiian cultural forms, wrote:

The sport of surfriding possessed a grand fascination, and for a time it seemed as if it had the vitality of its own as a national pastime. There are those living . . . who remember the time when almost the entire population of a village would at certain hours resort to the sea-side to indulge in, or to witness, this magnificent accomplishment. We cannot but mourn its decline. But this too has felt the touch of civilization, and to-day it is hard to find a surfboard outside of our museums and private collections.

Indeed, not unlike Hawaii's once plentiful birds and sea mammals, surfers had become an endangered species. Like the Hawaiian race in general, the sport was bobbing on a brink of extinction. Then, as the century turned, so did worldwide visions of Hawaii, and things Hawaiian.

Preceding pages: A 1920s study in Japanese ukiyo-e *wood block style of surfing at Waikiki. By the artist Charles William Bartlett.*

Below, an early 1920s water shot of surfers taking off on a fun, easy roller just Ewa of Diamond Head.

Preceding pages, the original Outrigger Canoe Club, ca. 1910; below, silent film star Betty Compson and beachboy extras.

"Wouldn't you like to be rescued this way," asked an Associated Press photo circulated on May 30, 1930.

Sport in the Surf, Honolulu.

During the early part of this century, folks on holiday at Waikiki could either sing or write home about their surfing experiences — as evidenced by the music sheet and hand-colored postcards on these pages.

SURF BOARD RIDING, HONOLULU, T. H.

ON THE BEACH AT WAIKIKI

WHERE BUT THE moment before was only the wide desolation and invincible roar, is now a man, erect, full-statured, not-struggling frantically in that wild movement, not buried and crushed and buffetted by those mighty monsters, but standing above them all, calm and superb, poised on the giddy summit, his feet buried in the churning foam, the salt smoke rising to his knees, and all the rest of him in the free air and flashing sunlight, and he is flying through the air, flying forward, flying fast as the surge on which he stands. He is a Mercury — a brown Mercury. His heels are winged, and in them is the swiftness of the sea..."

> — *Jack London*, in "A Royal Sport: Surfing at Waikiki," *1907*

When hard-drinking and chain-smoking Jack London first published his grand, purple prose about "a royal sport for the natural kings of earth," his purpose was to communicate a newly discovered wonder. Or, as he described it, the "ecstatic bliss" of riding one's first waves.

London's story first appeared as a travel piece in the October, 1907 issue of the *Woman's Home Companion*, then later, in 1911, was adapted as a chapter in his popular adventure book *The Cruise of the Snark*. At that tenuous point in time, surfing couldn't have wished for a more influential spokesman. Burly and brash, London was a best-selling literary lion, having only recently achieved international fame with adventure novels such as *The Call of the Wild* (1903), *The Sea-Wolf* (1904) and *White Fang* (1906). Indeed, in retrospect one could say that London did for the promotion of surfing what Ernest Hemingway would do in the 1940s for bullfighting and sportsfishing.

While in Waikiki during 1907, London and his wife, Charmian, lived in a bungalow at the Hau Tree Inn (now the Halekulani Regent Hotel), on rambling grounds just opposite Waikiki's most perfect surfing break, Number Threes. From there he was only a few minutes' walk from the then six-year-old Moana Hotel on Kuhio Beach. This stretch of sand was the daytime haunt of surf-riders, who numbered only a few in those days. There, under an old *hau* tree, and in and around the old Moana Bath House, he found the spiritual "ancestors" of today's famous Waikiki beachboys, the most obvious of that chang-a-lang gang being a loose clique of Hawaiians and part-Hawaiians who had formed a *hui*, or club, they called the Waikiki Swimming Club. This informal group was the precursor of two other beach clubs — the Outrigger Canoe Club and Hui Nalu ("Club of the Waves") — organized in 1908.

Also during his puttering about Waikiki, London made the acquaintance of two key characters in 20th Century surfing history. The first was Alexander Hume Ford, an eccentric journalist-wanderer who introduced London to the thrills of surfing. And second was the most celebrated surfer-beachboy of his time, a 23-year-old Irish-Hawaiian named George Freeth.

Ford, a puckish little chap who looked, in his own words, "like George Bernard Shaw," was an inveterate organizer. When he had a cause to sell, the first thing he would do is form an association or congress to achieve his goal. As an early newspaper account chuckled, "Ford was forming a club a month in those times."

Following several animated conversations with London, Ford decided to form the world's first properly chartered surfing organization, a beachside fraternity called the Outrigger Canoe and Surfboard Club. The Outrigger Club's main purpose, as stated in a fund-raising petition circulated by Ford in April, 1908, was "to give an added and permanent attraction to Hawaii and make Waikiki always the Home of the Surfer, with per-

NEPTUNE'S CHARGERS "BROKEN" BY MAN: RIDERS OF THE SURF.

DRAWN BY S. BEGG FROM A PHOTOGRAPH.

ON THE BOARD THAT WILL BEAR A MAN ONLY WHEN THE FORCE OF A WAVE IS BEHIND IT:
RIDING THE SURF.

Continued.

—Many, many times probably he will roll over, but at last the knack of balancing comes to him, and he is ready to try to stand upon his board while it is in full forward motion—not such a difficult feat after all, in the small surf where the waves are not more than two or three feet high at most. His real trials commence when he deserts the shallows and strikes out for the deep. It takes muscle and endurance, lying upon a bit of planking with only an inch or two of the bow above water, to paddle a mile out to where the waves form. There is half a minute of violent, then several seconds of supreme effort, the board begins to rise upon the wall of water, and then comes the fight to keep it from floating above the crest and sinking back in the rear—of a lost wave.'

Folks in merry old London town enjoyed this exciting vision of surfing over morning tea on September 10, 1910. It was early images and dispatches such as this one in The Illustrated London News *that ushered in surfing's "modern" era. Note the Royal Hawaiian crest on the surfer's bathing costume.*

A group of accommodating young Waikiki beach boys, right, stand at casual attention for a visitor's Kodak camera box. The muscular fellow at the center of this particular group is Dudie Miller, the popular first commodore of the Hui Nalu surf club.

haps an annual Surfboard and Outrigger Canoe Carnival which will do much to spread abroad the attractions of Hawaii, the only islands in the world where men and boys ride upright upon the crests of the waves."

Freeth, meanwhile, was *the* surfing star in turn of the century Waikiki and later in California. London credited first Ford, and then Freeth, with teaching him the finer points of surfing. It was in waves off Waikiki, during a Ford-arranged surfing lesson, that author London met waterman Freeth. Or as London describes that initial and casual encounter:

> Out there in the midst of such a succession of big smoky ones, a third man [besides him and Ford] was added to our party, one [George] Freeth. Shaking the water from my eyes as I emerged from one wave and peered ahead to see what the next one looked like, I saw him tearing in on the back of it, standing upright with his board, carelessly poised, a young god bronzed with sunburn. We went through the wave on the back of which he rode. Ford called to him. He turned an air spring from his wave, rescued his board from its maw, paddled over to us, and joined Ford in showing me things . . .

Probably as a direct result of London's highly complimentary and widely circulated surfing story, Freeth became this century's first "name" surfer. As a result, he was invited during 1907 to journey to California, at the expense of the sponsoring Redondo-Los Angeles Railway and industrialist Henry E. Huntington, to conduct public demonstrations of Hawaiian watersports. His West Coast promoters introduced him as an "aquatic attraction" and thus he became the first person known to ride a surfboard in California

Surf bathers
Waikiki beach Honolulu.

waves. So, inadvertently, he also became the "father" of California surfing.

Also frequenting Waikiki's waves during the time of London's 1907 stopover was then 13-year-old Duke Paoa Kahanamoku, who a few years later would astound the world with his record-shattering swimming exploits.

According to reliable beachside history, in 1908 organization man Ford approached the trustees of the Queen Emma Estate and petitioned them for a plot of land next to Waikiki's Moana Hotel. He wanted a place where a clubhouse and surfboard storage facilities could be built. An early newspaper report noted that he was encouraged by several influential people, including Jack and Charmian London, the filmmaker Burton Holmes and Honolulu socialite Ella Wheeler Wilcox. After a round of successful negotiations, Ford struck a deal with the former queen's trustees. Or, as he recalls in a memoir published in 1944 (a year before his death on October 14, 1945), "I got a 20 years lease on what is now the Outrigger Canoe Club grounds for $5 a year, provided the dues for boys under 16 would not be over $5 a year. I wish it were so now. Such dues made it possible for every kid with guts to live at least half the day fighting the surf."

Ford served as the Outrigger's first president, but he needed expert aquatic assistance once his organizational efforts had succeeded, so he invited a well-known Honolulu waterman, George D. Center, better known to three generations of Outrigger members as "Dad" Center, to become the club's first captain.

When I came to Hawaii in 1908 and formed the Outrigger club with the last dozen *haole* boys who could ride the surfboard, George D. Center was in his prime — the backbone and trainer of the Myrtle boat club. [But] he scorned the surf. It took me two years to persuade Dad to even come to Waikiki to take a look-see . . . [But] when I did get Center interested I was soon eclipsed — Dad could train the swimming teams, show the boys how to steer a canoe, ride a surfboard or train for a swimming contest.

Center, who coached Outrigger athletes for some 25 years, was best remembered as a swimming coach. He was the coach, for example, of America's team in the 1920 Olympics at Antwerp, and in 1927 he took the All-American Swimming Team to Japan for a series of competitive and exhibition meets. He was also known as the holder of Hawaii's unofficial long-distance surfing record, a distinction he earned in 1917 by riding a big summer wave all the way from distant Castle's Point to Waikiki proper. "Dad" Center — "the venerable old man of the Hawaiian sea" — died on September 12, 1962, at age 75.

Ford, innovative man that he was, also fathered other organizations — the Hawaiian Trail and Mountain Club (1910), the Hands-Around-the-Pacific Club (1911) and the Pan Pacific Union (1917), among others. He even started an unusual series of Good Relations clubs designed to foster understanding between Hawaii's various ethnic groups, and, somehow, he also found time to edit and publish a very creative travel and cultural periodical, the *Mid-Pacific Magazine*.

The Outrigger Club, however, was Ford's most enjoyable and enduring legacy. Since that beachside group's first two grass "clubhouses" were moved from the Honolulu Zoo and reconstructed at Kuhio Beach, it has since made three more location moves to accommodate its physical and financial growth. Its present posh and restrictive facilities on the Diamond Head side of Waikiki are a far cry from what the spartan Outrig-

This winsome "surfer girl" was the epitome of early surf chic. As her white, high-buttoned shoes hang a casual five, she smiles for sometime glamour photographer Ray Jerome Baker.

The famous Kahanamoku brothers, Dudie Miller, Pua Kealoha and Knute Cottrell are but a few of the surf classicists who appear in this important 1920s group portrait of Waikiki beachboys and 'beachgirls.'

ger used to be, but club members still excel in competitive watersports, and a certain surfside spirit survives. As a plaque mounted at the Club's entrance asks: "Let this be a place where man may commune with sun and sand and sea; and where the sports of Old Hawaii shall always have a home."

In 1911, three years after Ford and company registered the Outrigger Canoe and Surfboard Club, a group of swimmers and surfers headed by dissident Outrigger members W. A. (Knute) Cottrell, Duke Kahanamoku and Kenneth Winter organized and registered the Hui Nalu group as a swimming, canoeing and surfing club. Edward Kenneth Kaleleihealani (Dudie) Miller — an orchestra leader by night and one of Waikiki's top swimmers and surfers — was named Hui Nalu's commodore. The title of captain went to "the human fish," Duke Paoa Kahanamoku. The group's first president was William F. Rawlins. Honorary directors included Prince "Cupid" Kuhio Kalanianaole and Sanford B. Dole.

Hui Nalu's new H and N logo, and gold and black bathing costume soon rivaled the red Outrigger O and canoe paddle emblem for local surfside prestige. Hui Nalu's canoe teams soon began winning regattas "by hardly anything less than six to eight canoe lengths."

"And they were good at fund raising," recalls a recent Hui Nalu historical sketch. "Their Follies in 1914, staged by Ned Steele, Lew Henderson and Watson Ballentyne in the old Honolulu Opera House, had as patronesses Her Majesty Queen Liliuokalani, the Princess Kalanianaole, and notable matrons Mrs. Henry G. Smart, Mrs. Robert W. Shingle, Mrs. Walter Macfarlane, Mrs. George Beckley and others."

The new kama'āina beach club procured a locker room in the Moana Hotel, and charged its juvenile members $1 a year dues. "The status symbol of belonging to Hui Nalu was having a black clothes hook in that clubroom," a writer for The Honolulu Star-Bulletin said.

Hui Nalu's two greatest skippers during the past century were Dudie Miller and, in more recent years, Lukela "John D" Kaupiko. Both men were admired and loved for their leadership abilities and warm, outgoing dispositions.

When Dudie Miller died at age 49, on September 11, 1935, an obituary in The Honolulu Advertiser noted that his death "meant that one of Waikiki's most colorful figures was gone; that the man who has been father and guardian to the boys at the beach will never again come 'round with guiding words of counsel."

The story recalled that Miller was one of the Islands' best known musicians and probably Waikiki's premier beachboy.

"In 1912 he went to New York to play with his men in 'Bird of Paradise,' and was given an ovation of nine curtain calls at one performance . . . At Waikiki 'Dudie' was one of the first canoe steersmen to take out tourists for surfing parties and he was known in his prime as the best fisherman and surfer on the beach." The obituary reported that for Miller's final services "Hui Nalu members were preparing yesterday a huge flower surfboard, all of white ginger and with 'Dudie's' name spelled in yellow 'ilima."

Miller's successor, "John D" Kaupiko, was also a driving and inspirational captain. His peers nicknamed him "John D" because his kind manner was said to be as expansive as Rockefeller's purse. In the 1940s and 1950s, despite financial problems, Kaupiko guided his boys to seemingly impossible victories. During those years Hui Nalu's paddlers and surfers competed in a grand old canoe, Lio-keo-keo, a racing craft named after the dancing whitecaps on the waves off Waikiki's old Grays Beach.

Jude Miller. H. Nainoa. K. Cottrell. F. Wilhelm. Hilo Boyd. H. Coelle. D. Kahanamoku. Steamboat. H. Anahu.

H. Towa. Kim Wai. L. Kaupiko. J. Hjorth. Joe Fisher. W. Kahanamoku. Genoves. Holstein. Lewis. S. Kahanamoku. Leeda.

Poo Kealoha. Lady Langer. E. Gliebtrey. Stubby Kruger. Duke P. Kahanamoku. H. Prieste. H. Beckley. H. Awana.

This hand-colored and well-leied lass on a multi-stringered board promoted Hawaii in a 1930s magazine advertisement circulated by the Matson Navigation Company.

During the period from 1910 to 1950, the once dying sport of surfing surged back to life — partially as a result of good publicity, beginning with Jack London, but also because of Freeth and Kahanamoku, and the enthusiasm of clubs such as the Outrigger, Hui Nalu, Myrtle and Healani.

Also very influential during those early "modern surfing" years were a newly emerging breed of mainland surfers, so-called "coast haoles" who came to Hawaii on summertime holidays and learned surfing skills from that special group of Waikiki characters known collectively as beachboys. Until recently, most Hawaii-trained surfers learned the craft and practiced their first awkward surfing moves on the benign, easy-rolling waves of Waikiki. It is still probably the easiest place for a novice surfer to learn. Indeed, even Hawaii's most celebrated contemporary surfer, Gerry Lopez, rode his first waves at age 10 on a board his parents rented from a Waikiki beachboy.

Due to the languorous nature of their hang-loose "occupation," and also because of their basically sensuous and fun-loving ways, Waikiki's beachboys early on gained a reputation as partying fools and gigolo-like womanizers. Theirs was a naughty but nice mystique that survives, in a pleasantly laid-back style, to this day.

The local press loved — and still loves — to report the antics of Waikiki's beachboys. Consider a front-page story in *The Honolulu Advertiser* of March 10, 1926. Under a headline that read BEACH BOYS SLING "WICKED HOOF" TO WIN HONOLULU'S FIRST CHARLESTON CONTEST, writer "H.E.D." noted that Waikiki beachboy Bill Kahanamoku "is the 'Charleston King' of Honolulu today. He danced his way to $60 and local fame last night at the Hawaii theater."

Kahanamoku, H.E.D. said, won hands down with his "shimmy-clog-tango called the Charleston," but just as outrageous and popular was a second beachboy known to all as "Tough Bill."

"'Tough Bill' — we know of no other name for the popular beach guard — clowned his way to $25 and second place in the sun. 'Tough Bill' was dressed for the part — and the dress won for him, too," H.E.D. observed.

Both beachboys apparently strutted through phantom dancing, pantomime and comedy routines they dreamed up for the big social event. "Now and then the real negro eccentricity that makes the dance the rage of the mainland came to the fore. And when it did, one understood the dance's sweeping popularity," observed H.E.D.

Two years later, in 1928, an obviously stuffy visitor wrote a letter to *The Advertiser* in which the writer complained of alleged sexual activities being engaged in by Waikiki beachboys during the conduct of official beach-related business. That allegation by one "Puzzled Visitor" inspired a disgruntled beachboy, identified in print as "Surfrider," to pen an indignant rebuttal. In his letter-to-the-editor of April 13, 1928, besmirched "Surfrider" argued that "beach boys escort visiting ladies out in the surf at the ladies' request, and it is purely a business proposition." He clarified himself thusly:

> As I understood from the letter, Puzzled
> Visitor had been listening to remarks passed
> by other people on the Moana Pier to the
> effect that the three couples of beachboys
> and young women were bound for the 'outer
> reef or somewhere like that' and would there
> carry on their love making. Puzzled Visitor
> was badly misled and misinformed. Love
> making is most assuredly not done while on
> surf boards. The beach boys are on the
> beach for the purpose of making a living,
> which they do by giving surfing and
> swimming lessons, acting as life guards, and

Ladies and gentlemen, da boys. This vintage gathering of some of Waikiki's most memorable beachboys took place in 1962 on the occasion of the recording of a long play record album (Duke Kahanamoku Presents A Beachboy Party With Waltah Clarke). Pictured are (on the sand) Splash Lyons, Fat Kala and Panama Baptiste; (on the canoe) Squeeze Kamana, Ox, Jimmy Hakuole and Duke Kahanamoku; and (hovering in the background) producer Waltah Clarke, Kalakaua, Harry Robello and Chick Daniels.

giving visiting tourists and local people rides in outrigger canoes. Regular charges are made for services rendered outside of life guard duty. The party of three couples were going out to ride the waves; the ladies would be taught the technique of surfriding for which they would be charged. Just why such an incident should be called a 'novel spectacle' I am at a loss to understand. It is no more unusual or novel to see a boy and girl together on a surf board in Hawaii than it is to see them on a sled in snow time in the States!

So much for beachboy pride. But so it went, and so it still goes. Or as they say in Hawaii, "Beachboys will be beachboys."

Sarah Park, chief beachside and surfing correspondent for *The Honolulu Star-Bulletin* during the 1950s, recalled in one of her 1954 surfing columns that Waikiki's "Oldtime Beachboys" were a loosely knit lot, but every Christmas Day these elderly Hui Nalu, Outrigger, Myrtle, Healani and unaffiliated alumni of the sand would gather at Waikiki for an annual Beachcombers' Christmas Party. "At the latest gathering, held as always at the hau grove between the Outrigger and Moana," she wrote, "at least 200 oldtimers and not-so-old-timers met to bask in each other's company."

Miss Park reported that before going to the annual Christmas party, many of the senior beachboys — observing an unwritten protocol of their own — "tossed leis on the waters offshore" in memory of other beachboys who had died. Among attendees at that 1954 gathering were "characters" such as Louis "Sally" Hale, longtime manager of the Outrigger's beach services, and Chick Daniels, the Royal Hawaiian Hotel's beach captain known internationally for his hilarious pants-dropping hula called "da puka key." Other

surfside celebrities were Duke Kahanamoku, Splash Lyons, Toots Minvielle, Charles Amalu, Gay Harris, Steamboat Mokuahi, Panama Baptiste, William Hollinger, Blue Makua, Turkey Love and others too bashful to sit down for proper identification.

In one of her most memorable surfing columns for the *Star-Bulletin*, Miss Park suggested (on September 13, 1953) that a bored Honolulu hostess should "invite Waikiki's beach boys to partake of *your* board." "Introductions," she noted, "would go something like this:

"Hostess: 'Mrs. McWorkel, this is Turkey. He'll be seated on your left. And on your right we have another man from the beach, Sally.

"'And have you met Steamboat? And this is Steamboat Jr. [And] these are Steamboat's relatives: Tugboat, Sailboat, Lifeboat and Rowboat.

"'Of course you've met Dad. And here are Curly, Splash, Tarzan, Boss, Blue, Molokai, Keeaumoku, Panama Dave, Rabbit, Blackout, Wata, Zulu, Mungo, Eight-ball, Nose, Scooter Boy, [and] oh, here comes Dead-Eye.'"

Their zany nicknames were only one reflection of a beachboy style that has charmed Waikiki-goers for nearly a century. Indeed, what visitor to "the world's most famous beach" doesn't yearn for the good old days when the boys would go out and ride "beeg wahns" on their 10-foot and longer redwood surfboards.

A bit of that old-time silky shirt style was revived on June 4, 1977, when, in honor of the Honolulu Department of Parks and Recreation's 100th Anniversary, a special Sammy "Steamboat" Mokuahi Sr. Waikiki Beachboy Festival was held at Kuhio Beach. About a dozen of the 75 contestants in that surfing makahiki were beachboys from the Thirties era, and the guest of honor was — of course, brah — Steamboat himself. Steamboat's nickname, by the way, is a free translation of his

Tom Blake of Wisconsin poses with six of the surfboards he crafted during his surfing years at Waikiki. The four at left are hollowed-out reproductions of ancient Hawaiian 'olo surfboards, and the two at right are paddleboards of his own design.

last name, Mokuahi. *Moku* means "vessel," and *ahi* means fire; hence, the "fire vessel," or a steamboat.

Honolulu Advertiser reporter Peter Rosegg captured the spirit of that nostalgic Steamboat meet in a fine story titled "Surfboards and Memories." A typical vignette:

At age 68, Clarence Kano was probably the oldest ex-beachboy in competition. He started working for "Dad" Center in 1927, he said, but quit more than 30 years ago to go into the trucking business. Then, a few years ago, he started surfing again. "I guess it's just in me," he said.

"Eh, Kano, you die like a rat," one of his friends yelled to him, and all the other beachboys laughed. "It means that when I fall off the board I sink," Kano explained with a grin. "I have to scramble all around to find the board and get back on."

Those were indeed da days, brah, and it was into such a strange milieu that a mild-mannered *haole* from Wisconsin ventured one sunny day in 1924. His name was Tom Blake, and he was in Hawaii on a pilgrimage of sorts. Or to use a more contemporary term, he was on *surfari.*

Blake's more than usual interest in surfing was inspired by the swimmer Duke Kahanamoku in, of all places, Detroit. It was there in 1920 that Blake chanced to meet the Duke. Kahanamoku was stopping over in Detroit on his way back home from a successful showing at that year's Olympiad at Antwerp, and he and a group of fellow Hawaiian swimmers went out to a Detroit movie house to watch themselves swim in a talkie newsreel show.

"I, too, had come to see the film — and I was so impressed when I found myself near this champion that I intercepted him in the theater lobby and asked to shake his hand," Blake wrote years later.

Blake recalls that the congenial Kahanamoku so influenced him that he vowed to make swimming his avocation. He went into training as an amateur swimmer, and later that year, after having moved to California, began working out at the old Los Angeles Athletic Club. He practiced hard and became so adept a waterman that in the fall of 1922, at age 22, he won a first-place medal in the ten-mile swim at an AAU meet at Philadelphia. Two years later he moved to Honolulu and began a long career — in both Hawaii and California — as a surfer and surfing innovator.

Blake's contributions to surfing are landmarks. By applying common sense and an enthusiastic desire to make surfboard paddling and surfing more fun, Blake revolutionized the sport.

One of the first things he did was "accidentally" invent the first hollow surfboard, an innovation which, in turn, led to the first hollow paddleboard. This occurred in 1926 when Blake was trying to duplicate an ancient Hawaiian surfing board he had studied in Honolulu's Bernice Pauahi Bishop Museum. Blake recalls that, "Strange as it may seem, three old-style Hawaiian surfboards of huge dimensions and weight have hung on the walls of the Bishop Museum in Honolulu for twenty years or more without anyone doing more than wonder how in the world these great boards were used, and were they not too long and heavy to be practicable.

"I, too, wondered about these boards in the museum, wondered so much that in 1926 I built a duplicate of them as an experiment, my object being to find not a better board, but to find a faster board to use in the annual and popular surfboard paddling races held in Southern California each summer."

Blake's own handwritten notes outline bits of surfing history, right, on a page of his important source book, Hawaiian Surfboard, *1913. The tipped in snapshot, photographer unknown, captures the start of the first official surfing contest ever held in California.*

In a personally annotated copy of his classic surfing book *Hawaiian Surfboard*, published in 1935 by Paradise of the Pacific Press of Honolulu, Blake notes (in his own handwriting) that he took this duplicate board and, on a whim, "drilled it full of holes to lighten & dry it out, then plugged them [the holes] up. Result: accidental invention of the first hollow surf-board."

Blake's experimentation continued, and by 1928 he was ready to demonstrate the hollow board's capabilities. His initial public showing took place in 1928 at the first Pacific Coast Surf-riding Championships, held that year at Corona Del Mar on the east side of Newport Bay. He remembers that he and his 16-foot, 120 pound board drew snickers from the other California surfers as he lugged it down to the water.

"When I appeared with it for the first time before 10,000 people gathered for a holiday and to watch the races, it was regarded as silly," Blake said. "Handling this heavy board alone, I got off to a poor start, the rest of the field gaining a thirty-yard lead in the meantime. It really looked bad for the board and my reputation and hundreds openly laughed. But a few minutes later it turned to applause because the big board led the way to the finish of the 880-yard course by fully 100 yards."

Blake emerged from the surf triumphant, and his reputation as an inventive and keenly competitive waterman grew even stronger. Encouraged by his success, Blake in 1930 acquired a patent — U.S. Patent Number 1872230 — for his "Hawaiian Hollow Surfboard" and began promoting it as both a wave-riding and lifesaving watercraft. His first 1930 model was manufactured by the Thomas N. Rogers Company of Venice, California, and a later 1940 version was manufactured by the Los Angeles Ladder Company.

In Hawaii, where Blake's surfing peers referred to his invention as "Blake's cigar," the board created a bit of a controversy in purist Hawaiian surfing circles. Longtime Waikiki champion surfer/paddler Sam Reid recalls, in a detailed surfing memoir, published in 1955 in *The Honolulu Star-Bulletin*, that Blake and his cigar board set new records in both the 100-yard and half-mile paddling events of the Hawaiian Surfboard Paddling Championships of January 1, 1930.

"However," Reid wrote, "it was a 'hollow' victory, for Blake had hollowed out his 16-foot cigar-board to a 60 pound weight, compared with an average 100 to 125 pounds weight of the other 9 boards in the 100."

Reid said that many of the "purist" Hawaiian surfers and distance paddlers of that time cried "foul," and demanded that any future paddling contests be held only on traditionally shaped and solid surfboards. Other paddlers lobbied for the hollow "cigar board," claiming, rightfully, that it "marked the beginning of a new era in surfing and paddling." Or as Reid wrote:

Reverberations of the "hollow board" tiff were heard from one end of the Ala Wai to the other and echoes can still be heard at Waikiki even today — 25 years later. At a meeting of the three [surfing] clubs, Outrigger, Hui Nalu and Queens, held immediately after the disputed races [of 1930], it was decided that henceforth there would be no limit whatever on [the design] of paddleboards. . . .

Within a year, Reid said, surfboard builders were experimenting with all sorts of sizes, shapes, weights and materials, including airplane fabric boards, canvas boards, hydroplane bottoms and converted single sculls. "Imagination of design," he remembers, "ran riot."

scattered from coast to coast.

(1947 - The war
stopped mfg. and
much of the use of
-boards in the U.S.A.
although a few were
used for war
purposes.
T.E.B.

Tom Blake

RLDS ORIGINAL HOLLOW BOARD.
⊕ TOM BLAKE - BUILT IN
1926.

START - 1ST ANNUAL PACIFIC COAST
SURFING CONTEST -
BALBOA - CALIF. 1928.

75

↗↑ The long white board above was the first
reproduction of the ancient Hawaiian OLO
chiefs board - however it was hollow to
lighten it - Duke Kahanamoku
also rode this board. Thos. Blake

83

Matson Line to Hawaii

NEW ZEALAND · AUSTRALIA VIA SAMOA · FIJI

There are so many reasons to be happy in *Hawaii*

Complete details of fascinating Matson Cruises through the South
Pacific from all Travel Agents or Matson Line-Oceanic Line, New York,
Chicago, San Francisco, Los Angeles, San Diego, Seattle, Portland.

*Hawaiian hotel reservations, at the beautiful Royal Hawaiian and Moana on
Waikiki Beach, can now be made at the same time you book your steamer passage.*

S. S. LURLINE · S. S. MARIPOSA · S. S. MONTEREY · S. S. MALOLO

*Natural color photograph
taken at Waikiki Beach*
© MATSON NAVIGATION CO., 1937

84

During the 1930s, surfing enjoyed a wholesome, boy-meets-girl image, as evidenced by a happy Matson ad, opposite page, and left on the December 15, 1938 cover of Vogue magazine. This unusual cover study was shot by the celebrated documentary and fashion photographer Toni Frissell. She snapped it from a specially built scaffold she had built and mounted astride two Waikiki outrigger canoes. Ms. Frissell's cover shot is reproduced courtesy of Vogue, The Condé Nast Publications Inc. and The Library of Congress.

4

TO 1

HONOLULU HAWAII

HAWAII

DUKE KAHANAMOKU
CHAMPION SWIMMER OF THE WORLD

THE DUKE: SURFING'S 'FATHER'

THE MONTH was August, of 1911, and on the U.S. Mainland, far from Hawaii, Amateur Athletic Union officials did not believe what they were being told — that a relatively unknown, 21-year-old Hawaiian named Duke Kahanamoku had just broken the world's most important swimming record by thrashing through 100 yards of saltwater in an amazing 55.4 seconds.

And what they found even more unbelievable were the circumstances: Kahanamoku, they were informed, had not *just* shattered the 100-yard sprint mark. He did it in Honolulu Harbor, on a straightaway course that stretched from a barnacled old barge into what was called the Alakea Slip, a moorage between Piers 6 and 7. A thick rope was stretched taut over the water to mark the finish line.

A 55.4 seconds showing in the 100-yard sprint? In a murky, flotsam-filled harbor? Between two ships' piers? I mean, really folks?

The reply that the incredulous AAU officials sent back on the wireless to Honolulu is a classic. "What," their telegram asked, "are you using for stop watches? Alarm clocks?!"

The meet in question was the first officially sanctioned AAU swimming and diving competition ever held in Hawaii, and the judges and other officials were experienced and certified. But who could believe Duke's showings that day? Besides his 55.4 second time in the 100-yard sprint, a time that bettered by 4.6 seconds the world record held by then two-time U.S. Olympic champion Charles M. Daniels, Duke also tied Daniels' world record of 24.2 seconds in the 50-yard freestyle, and, for extra measure, he outswam all competitors with a respectable 2:42.4 second finish in the 220-yard freestyle event.

Journalists covering that meet recall that the five timers on duty were so amazed that they ordered the Honolulu Harbor course remeasured —

not once, but four times. For good measure they even brought in a professional surveyor.

Everything matched up and timed out, and all Hawaii cheered. The next morning *The Honolulu Advertiser* proclaimed: "Duke Kahanamoku Broke Two Swimming Records. Hawaiian Youth Astounds People By The Way He Tore Through The Water."

The reporter who covered the event for *The Advertiser* said that two American Amateur Swimming records were broken yesterday by Duke Kahanamoku, the expert natatorial member of the Hui Nalu Club. "Kahanamoku," he exclaimed, "is a wonder, and he would astonish the mainland aquatic spots if he made a trip to the coast."

However, when the results of the Hawaii meet were officially submitted to the New York AAU officials, they refused to acknowledge what had happened and disapproved Duke's times. They argued that Duke's record-breaking swims were aided by a strong-flowing current in Honolulu Harbor! Years later they had to retract, but it was late by then.

Officials and fans in Honolulu were dismayed when they received the news, but Kahanamoku, easy-going son of a Honolulu police captain, simply smiled a big Hawaiian smile and dove back into training. Years later he told a Honolulu reporter that he was able to swim so fast in Honolulu Harbor because "Our water is so full of life, it's the fastest water in the world. That's all there is to it."

Duke Paoa Kahinu Mokoe Hulikohola Kahanamoku — known to most folks as Duke or The Duke, and as Paoa to Hawaiian and longtime island friends — was used to such skepticism. Nobody would believe he was as good as he was. Two years earlier, at 19, he was already breaking swimming records. Usually, however, those "unofficial" showings were simply filed away alongside an asterisk and regarded as "curious."

King Gustaf applauds and Duke smiles after His Royal Highness awarded Kahanamoku a gold medal for his 1912 Olympic win of the 100-meter sprint.

But when Duke finally got a chance to splash his stuff for the "big time," that is outside Hawaii, he did so quietly but impressively. When he made it to the Mainland, he delighted sports fans with his swimming technique he had learned from Australian swimmers who visited Hawaii in 1910. This new swimming style, which sportswriters called "the Kahanamoku Kick," was Duke's home-grown version of the Australian Crawl. He had a natural bent for speed swimming, and his "flutter kick" gave him the extra edge he needed to become a world champion. Honolulu sports columnists used to joke that Kahanamoku's "luau feet" were so big (size 13) they literally propelled him through the water.

Once he got used to colder Mainland water, the Duke's performances were dazzling. Sports fans began to call him "The Human Fish" and "The Bronze Duke of Waikiki." After warm-up meets in Chicago and Pittsburgh, among other places, Duke competed in an Olympic trials swimming meet held during May, 1912, at Philadelphia. He qualified for the U. S. Olympic team by winning the 100 meters freestyle event in exactly 60 seconds.

Less than a month later, at Verona Lake, N. J., he qualified for the U. S. Olympic 800-meter relay team, but, more important, during his 200-meter "test" heat, he bettered the existing world record in the 200-meter freestyle that had been held by the aforementioned Daniels. Though he wasn't considered a middle distance swimmer, he bested Daniels' 200-meter record by six-tenths of a second. His time: 2:40.0.

A reporter who covered the Verona Lake meet for the *New York World* noted that Kahanamoku got off to an "unconcerned" start, "and it was fully two seconds before he went after the field. Once in the water, he quickly overhauled his opponents." Following those trials, Duke—and fellow American athletes who had qualified for the 1912 Olympiad—steamed off for Stockholm.

Duke recalled in later years that it was while on that team shipbound for Sweden that he made the acquaintance of another "native" American who had qualified for the Games. The other fellow was Jim Thorpe, an American Indian who had become an All-America football player—while playing for the Carlisle (Pa.) Indian School team—and who was celebrated as the greatest all-around athlete of his time.

"When Jimmy and I were on the boat to the Olympics in Sweden," Duke remembered, "we had a talk. I said, 'Jimmy, I've seen you run, jump, throw things and carry the ball. You do everything so why don't you swim too?'

"Jimmy just grinned at me with that big grin he had for everyone, and said, 'Duke, I saved that for you to take care of. I saved that for you.' "

What followed in Stockholm was sports history of the grandest sort. Thorpe won almost everything on land, Kahanamoku won almost everything in the water, and these two aboriginal athletes, the Irish-Algonquin from Oklahoma, and the Hawaiian "Duke" from Hawaii, became the toast of the Olympics and the world.

In his first credentials-establishing appearance in the 100-meter freestyle swim (on July 6), Duke broke Daniels' world record in that event by a full three seconds. He later cruised to a gold medal in the finals of that event. He probably would have set yet another world record, but he was late off his starting block, and at the 80-meter mark slowed down a bit when he craned his head and looked back to see how far behind his competitors were.

Kahanamoku and Thorpe so impressed their Swedish hosts—and the world—that both were personally called to the Royal Victory Stand where they received their gold medals and Olympic wreaths directly from Sweden's King Gustaf.

Hawaii's 'Bronze Duke of Waikiki' was for most of this century a favorite portrait subject of visiting professional and amateur photographers. At left he poses with his personally inscribed 'Duke' redwood board and in a swimming tank top inscribed with the 'HN' of the famous Hui Nalu Hawaiian surf club.

Duke scratches his head in mock amazement, and his cycling bruddahs smile as they receive a "too many passengers" and speeding ticket in downtown Honolulu. This humorous publicity shot was taken during the 1920s and was widely circulated by the News of Hawaii photo agency.

In 1965, during a 75th birthday interview with Fran Reidelberger of *The Honolulu Star-Bulletin*, the Duke reminisced about that triumphant moment 53 years earlier.

"Come here. Come here a minute. Let me show you something," he said to Reidelberger. She recalls that the Duke's "now cloudy eyes became clear and his halting speech fluent as he fondly handled a framed wreath on his bedroom wall.

" 'I was just a big dumb kid when King Gustaf of Sweden gave me this. I didn't even know what it was really and almost threw it away. But now it is my most prized trophy,' he said proudly."

Prized indeed, and when Duke returned to the United States that year he was besieged by adoring sports fans and reporters. Wherever he went, "The Swimming Duke" was feted like visiting royalty. Perhaps it was his unusual first name, or maybe it was his striking good looks, but wherever he traveled, a certain respectful elegance surrounded this quiet young waterman from Waikiki.

Early reports from the U. S. Mainland and the Continent told of journalistic attempts to link The Duke to royal Hawaiian origins, but whenever reporters would ask Duke about his family, he'd say simply, "My father is a policeman." His father, Captain Kahanamoku, was born in the Hawaiian Princess Ruth's palace during the visit to Hawaii in 1869 of England's Duke of Edinburgh. So in honor of that royal visit Duke's mother named him Duke. He in turn passed the name on to a son born on August 24, 1890.

For months following his Olympic victories in Europe, Duke swam in exhibitions and swimming meets throughout Europe and the United States. It was while on these tours that he began to demonstrate, among other aquatic techniques, his prowess in the ancient Hawaiian sport of surfing. In places such as Atlantic City, and Corona Del Mar, California, crowds gathered and cheered as Duke surfed expertly on glassy morning waves. Except for a few folks who had seen earlier surfing exhibitions in Southern California by George Freeth, most Coast *haoles* had never seen such a fascinating use of maritime energy.

Largely as a result of the Duke's much ballyhooed exhibitions on the West and East coasts, the then exotic sport of surfing began to attract a dedicated cult following. The Duke also caught the eye of Hollywood, that then young enclave of moviemakers in the Los Angeles area. He was asked to play parts in early films being produced there. As early as 1913 he was hanging out with Hollywood's beautiful people during the week, and taking certain of these new friends surfing on weekends.

Duke stayed in the Los Angeles area off and on for twenty years. "I played chiefs — Polynesian chiefs, Aztec chiefs, Indian chiefs . . . all kinds of chiefs," he once said. He also did bits as "a Hindu thief and an Arab prince." It wasn't until 1948 that he played a Polynesian. His film name was *Ua Nuka*, or "the Big Rain," and he was cast opposite that great white hunter, John "Duke" Wayne, in a movie titled "*The Wake of the Red Witch.*"

All these years the Duke's fame continued to spread. In 1915 he took his swimming and surfing skills to Australia. Oldtimers there recall that his appearances in New South Wales, under the auspices of the Australian Swimming Association, caused quite a stir in surfbathing circles. The Duke literally pushed that great sea-oriented country into surfing.

As early as 1912, a first surfboard had been imported to Australia by a C. D. Patterson of Sydney, but, according to Aussie sources, that nine-foot-long redwood slab ended up in the Patterson household as "an ironing board." During the next couple of years other inventive Australians attempted to duplicate what they *thought* were Ha-

waiian surfboards, but it wasn't until Duke was invited to visit Australia that proper surfing was observed in Oz.

Duke's first coming to Australia created a lot of excitement. Cecil Healy, a would-be surfer and writer of that time, wrote in 1914:

> Kahanamoku is a wonderfully dexterous performer on the surfboard, an instrument of pleasure that Australians have so far been unsuccessful in handling to any degree. Reports have been brought back from overseas of his acrobatic feats executed while dashing shorewards at great speeds, but one doubts the possibility of Duke, or anyone else, duplicating such feats in Australian surf. Still, if he should give one of his rare exhibitions for our edification, be sure it will create a keen desire on the part of our ambitious shooters to emulate his deeds, and it goes without saying that his movements will be watched intently. Personally, I am convinced that the natural amphibious attitude of the Australians will enable one or another to unravel the knack.

Patricia Gilmore, an Australian reporter-historian, wrote in a 1948 nostalgia piece published by *The Sydney Morning Herald* that once Duke arrived in Australia he was asked to give an exhibition of surfboard riding. And, as she recalls:

> Having no board, he picked out some sugar pine from George Hudson's, and made one. This board — which is now in the proud possession of Claude West — was eight feet six inches long, and concave underneath. Veterans of the waves contend that Duke purposely made the surfboard concave instead of convex to give him greater stability in our rougher (as compared with Hawaiian) surf.

Duke Kahanamoku was asked to select the beach where the exhibition would be given. He chose Freshwater (now Harbord). It was in February, 1915, that Australian board enthusiasts had their first opportunity of seeing a 'board expert' on the waves. There was a big sea running, and from 10:30 in the morning until 1 o'clock Duke never left the water.

He showed the watchers all the tricks he knew, sliding right across the beach on the face of a wave. Demonstrating the ease with which he could manage with a passenger, he took Isabel Letham (still a resident at Harbord) out with him, and they would come right into the beach with incomparable grace and precision.

Thus the ancient Hawaiian sport of *he'enalu* was unveiled grandly in Australia. Concurrent with surfing's Duke-inspired development in California, this "new" recreation form took off on both sides of the Pacific Ocean. Today, surfing is a national mania Down Under, where it vies respectably with rugby, horse racing and beer drinking as the most *too right* thing to do in Aussie-land.

Probably few young people in Australia are aware of Duke's 1914–1915 swimming and surfing exploits in their country, but old-timers remember his impact. In 1939, on the eve of a big Pacific Aquatic Carnival held in Honolulu, a then longtime surfboard champion of Australia, Snowy McAlister, wrote: "We in Australia learned the rudiments of the sport from Duke. He gave the boards new meanings. I don't think anybody, Hawaiian or Australian, could duplicate Duke's old time skill."

Because of the outbreak of World War I, no Olympiad was held in 1916, so Duke busied him-

Duke, Down Under's special guest of honor, poses with hosts at a Sydney-area beach house during his historic 1915 visit to Australia. The Duke's influence on watersports and surfing in that country was formidable.

A natty Duke joins a visiting shtick artist, Groucho Marx, in a bit of hoomalimali. Indeed, when Hollywood came to Hawaii, he or she first called on Hawaii's Duke.

self training American Red Cross volunteers in water lifesaving techniques. With a group of American aquatic champions, he also went on tour with the Red Cross, swimming in sports exhibitions designed to raise money for America's war casualties. Once again, as part of his "act," Duke turned both American coasts on to surfing. California oldtimers recall "catching the waveriding bug" after only one look at the visiting Duke on his big redwood surfing board.

American surfing pioneer Tom Blake noted that Duke's surfing exploits at Ocean City, New Jersey, and Nassau, New York, during the 1910s marked the birth of East Coast surfing. "The present-day growth of surfing along the East Coast of the United States can be considered, in part, an extension of the demonstrations that Duke Kahanamoku made — (that) waves of the Atlantic as well as the Pacific provided all the power a surfer needed for riding."

Blake also comments on the progressive surfing style then being popularized by the Duke:

> It is good to recall the kind of surfing that Duke demonstrated in those times and places. It was not just the old traditional riding straight ahead before the break, toward shore. He, as well as other pioneers of the early 1900s at Waikiki, had developed skill at angling and sliding toward the right or left along the face of the advancing wave. And this at a time when the boards did not have a fixed fin or skeg to help with steering and stabilizing!

It was also during this period that Duke and George "Dad" Center of the Outrigger Canoe Club negotiated some of the biggest and longest rides of their lives in the surfing grounds off usually placid Waikiki. Stories about those rides, during the summer of 1917, have been given almost a "legendary" status, but are worth repeating at least in part.

As Waikiki tradition recalls, one beautiful summer day a rare outer surfing lineup called Castle's Surf — or Zero Surf — had begun building on the outermost reefs. Huge swells, called "bluebirds" by Duke and other old-time surfers, were lifting. These "bluebirds," reportedly generated by a strong earthquake in Japan, were, in turn, pushed up to their maximum height by strong summer tradewinds. In later years, Duke estimated the height of those swells as 30-foot-plus. Nobody will ever know for sure how big the waves were, but for years afterward Waikiki beachboys raved about the awesome rides Duke and Center completed that day. The distances they traveled — from takeoff point to beachside finish — were estimated to be at least half a mile.

Whatever the exact navigational circumstances, Duke commented later that, "I never caught another wave anything like that one. And now with the birthdays piled up on my back, I know I never shall. Nobody will ever take the memory away from me. It is a golden one that I treasure, and I'm grateful that God gave it to me."

In 1920, at the Olympic Games at Antwerp, Duke again distinguished himself as "the world's fastest swimmer." He broke his previous world record in the 100-meter sprint with a time of 60.4 seconds. He also swam on the winning U. S. 800-relay team with fellow Hawaiian Pua Kealoha, and Norman Ross and Perry McGillivray of Chicago.

"When the 1920 games at Antwerp, Belgium, rolled round, many thought that Duke at 30 was a bit too old to try out for the American team. But at the behest of Dad Center he whipped back into shape and defended his Olympic crown in a new world record time," recalled Honolulu sports columnist Red McQueen.

It wasn't until 1924 — during that year's Paris Olympiad — that the swimming Duke was dethroned. The first-place winner that year was one of his best friends, a young speedster from the Illinois Athletic Club named Johnny Weismuller. Hawaii, however, was more than proud that year, because the second-placing Duke, by then 34, brought home the 100-meter event's silver medal — and a younger brother, Sam, won the event's third-place bronze.

The Duke's by then legendary status in sports history had already been established, but a year later, while he was in Southern California working on another motion picture, the Duke achieved even greater renown as a hero.

On June 14, 1925, Duke was at Newport Beach enjoying a picnic with a group of Hollywood actors and actresses. Offshore, unusually big waves were pounding.

Suddenly, someone ran up the beach, calling for lifeguards. A pleasure yacht, the *Thelma*, with 29 on board, had capsized in the rough seas. Immediately Duke headed out into the surf with his 114-pound surfboard and began rescuing people. He paddled out and back several times, each time rescuing more victims. Of the 29 persons on the *Thelma*, 17 died. But of the 12 who survived, eight were rescued by Duke and his surfboard.

Southern California never forgot the incident. Years later, in a front page story about the Duke's life, *Los Angeles Times* reporter Dial Torgerson wrote: "His role on the beach that day was more dramatic than the scores he played in four decades of intermittent bit-part acting in Hollywood films. For one thing, that day he was the star."

Even though he was growing older, Duke continued to qualify for Olympic competition. In 1932, at 42, he qualified as a member of the U. S. Olympic water polo team that competed in that year's Los Angeles Games. He was well past the

age when any man would even consider entering such grueling competition, but as he said later: "I wanted to see if I could still swim. I didn't do too well . . . (but) I guess you begin to slow down a little when you get around 40."

Following that Olympiad, the Duke returned to Hawaii and sought new career opportunities. For a while, he operated two Union Oil Company service stations, one in Waikiki, and the other in the Pauoa/Nuuanu area of Honolulu. "It was something to do," he said. Then, in 1936, he went into politics and was elected to the office of Sheriff of the City and County of Honolulu. He was re-elected to this post for 13 straight terms.

"But what he lost in his post as sheriff he quickly regained in recognition of his years of unofficial service as an ambassador of goodwill. He was made Official Greeter for the City-County," *The Honolulu Star-Bulletin* reported that year.

During those twilight years, when a man is supposed to be slowing down, Duke remained active, traveling throughout the United States as a "symbol of Hawaii." Many people, even close friends, forgot that he had suffered from a serious heart attack in 1955, and that in 1962 he was treated for a cerebral blood clot and gastric ulcers.

During 1965, his 75th year, his personal and "ambassadorial" activities included the following:

For openers, he was the first person inducted into both the swimming and surfing Halls of Fame established that year. At the Swimming Hall of Fame he was reunited with "younger" swimming greats such as Johnny (Tarzan) Weismuller and fellow Honolulu swimmer-actor Buster Crabbe. And when a Surfing Hall of Fame was instituted by *International Surfing* magazine that year at Santa Monica, Duke was the first member — and most honored guest.

Surfers who attended the Surfing Hall of Fame ceremonies on June 17, 1965 at the Santa Monica Civic Auditorium, will recall that some 2,000 famous surfers and surfing industry celebrities rose in unison to give Duke a standing ovation as he arrived to take his place at the opening ceremonies. Following that grand evening, *International Surfing* dedicated its August-September issue to Duke, calling him "a surfer who by all standards is king."

In September of that year he was, for the third straight year, the guest of honor of Huntington Beach, California, at the United States Surfing Championships. Then in December, he was honored when the first Duke Kahanamoku Invitational Surfing Championships were held at Sunset Beach on Oahu in nearly wondrous wave conditions. That event, which one surfing publication described as "surfing's greatest competitive event ever" was the first truly professional and prestigious meet ever held in radical and challenging Hawaiian surf. It featured, by invitation, 24 of the world's finest surfers and was broadcast on Easter Sunday of 1966 as a CBS Sports Spectacular. It was estimated that some 40 to 50 million people, the greatest television audience ever for a surfing contest to that date, watched the show. That show — produced by filmmaker Larry Lindbergh and the contest's creator, Kimo Wilder McVay — later received a nomination for a prestigious Emmy award as one of the best special sports productions aired during 1966.

And the Duke beat went on. In April of 1966, Duke and Hawaii surfing champions Paul Strauch, Jr. and Fred Hemmings, Jr. traveled to Houston, to be honored guests at the first Houston-Hawaii Surfing Week. As guests of the city, the Hawaii trio made numerous public appearances, and were even feted at the National Aeronautics and Space Administration's (NASA) headquarters as official guests of America's first astronauts.

The following month, "Mister Pipeline," the

The year is 1965, and Hawaii's ambassadorial Duke takes time out to pose with his surf team, including (from left) surfing greats Paul Strauch, Jr., Joey Cabell, Fred Hemmings and Butch "Mr. Pipeline" Van Artsdalen.

PAUL STRAUCH, JR.   JOEY CABELL   THE DUKE   FRED HEMMINGS

BUTCH
VAN ARTSDALEN

late and fondly regarded Butch Van Artsdalen, joined Duke's group in Southern California during a massive Broadway department stores "Salute to Hawaii" promotion and tour. Duke, Butch, Fred and Paul made appearances at 20 major shopping centers in what was said to have been "the biggest department store promotion ever arranged on behalf of Hawaii merchandise."

During that visit, Duke and his team of surfing greats made a memorable visit to Malibu's famed surfing beach. On a day every gremmie within miles will never forget, the Duke and Company arrived at Malibu in a vintage Rolls Royce with surfboards strapped onto its top. That Hollywood-style surfari got nationwide television coverage and, with a wink, the Duke told his network interviewer, "My boys and I, we showed 'em how to go surfing."

Jim Murray, *The Los Angeles Times'* surfing columnist emeritus, interviewed Duke during that visit and commented: "I don't know who the greatest athlete of the half-century was, but I know who one of them was — a great, lion-headed old man I spoke to, between dozes, at the Ambassador the other afternoon."

Murray recalled that when President John F. Kennedy visited Hawaii in 1962, he walked past many of the island politicians on hand to greet the Duke, one of his childhood heroes.

"Kennedy was passing curtly along the line of dreary politicians," wrote Murray, "when he suddenly came upon Duke. A big, broad grin spread over the President's features, and the two men . . . had a long lively discussion of the crawl stroke and flutter-kick pioneered by Duke."

The Queen Mother of England was so charmed by Duke when she met him at Honolulu Airport in May of 1966 that she shed Royal decorum and danced an impromptu hula with him. How the flashbulbs popped, and the next morning Hawaii's Duke and Britain's Queen Mother were featured on many an international front page.

At age 75, Duke crowned beauty queens, attended banquets, was profiled by *Sports Illustrated*, helped land a marlin at Hawaii's annual Billfish Tournament in Kona, appeared on Ed Sullivan's TV show and Arthur Godfrey's radio show, chatted with columnist Walter Winchell, was named an honorary district commodore in the United States Coast Guard, and was the recipient of Hawaii's first Medicare card.

On his 75th birthday *The Honolulu Advertiser* said in a special editorial that "Few areas in the world have been as blessed as Hawaii with a man like Duke Kahanamoku as a symbol of vigorous achievement and friendly goodwill." The editorial went on:

Today, at 75, Duke Kahanamoku has been our best-known citizen for so long that the only real question for history is how big his legend will become. Some of the things bearing his name include a foundation, a beach, a swimming pool at the university, an annual regatta, a restaurant and nightspot, a line of sportswear, a music and recording corporation, a new line of tennis shoes, ukuleles, skateboards and surfboards, a surfing club and an international surfing championship sponsored by the CBS television network. In varying ways, each of these attests to the esteem in which this man is held not only throughout our nation but throughout the world . . .

On January 22, 1968, Hawaii's most famous citizen, and the century's "Father of Surfing," died of a heart attack at Honolulu's Waikiki Yacht Club. *Auwē*, the world mourned. The beloved Duke of Hawaii was dead.

Ron Stoner, who probably more than any other photographer captured the "mood" of surfing during the 1960s, took this fine portrait of Duke during the 1966 World Surfing Championships held that year in the San Diego area. On the following pages, paddleboarders race to the finish during a 1933 surf contest at Venice, California.

A CULT IS BORN

SHOULD YOU happen to go for a stroll on the board-walk at Redondo Beach one of these days, ask a local to show you the bust there of George Freeth. Chances are that he or she — surfer or not — won't know what you're talking about.

But, yes, there it is — a somewhat inconspicuous but formal monument to an Irish-Hawaiian beachboy who was the first person to turn California on to surfing, and vice-versa. An inscription below Freeth's bust identifies him as the man who "revived the lost Polynesian art of surfing" and as the man "who can walk on water."

Duke Kahanamoku (1912) probably had a more glamorous and far-reaching impact on early surfboard riding in the Golden State, but it was Freeth (1907) who pioneered the sport there. Freeth, the "Brown Mercury" described by Jack London in his important magazine feature and book chapter about surfing at Waikiki, was imported from Hawaii by the Los Angeles-based Pacific Electric Railway to promote its Los Angeles-Redondo Beach spur line. Shortly after his arrival in Southern California, midst grandly orchestrated press notices and other such "step right up, folks" public relations, then 23-year-old Freeth began wowing West Coast beachgoers with demonstrations of surfing on an eight-foot long redwood surfing craft. His hitherto unknown "Hawaiian feats" first took place during the spring of 1907 at Redondo Beach, but soon he began taking "his act" up and down the California coast, notably to virgin surf spots such as Balboa Beach to the south and Palos Verdes farther north.

"Freeth's daring performances," recalls an early California promotional piece, "attracted many visitors to the Southland each week-end; and they stood in awe and amazement, witnessing the spectacle of a man STANDING on the water.

"Not long after the original introduction of this sport, he took upon himself three proteges, 'Pink' Furlong, 'Sid' Williams, and 'Lou' Martin, the latter two of whom mastered the art and assisted him in many of the aquatic performances which he originated for the entertainment of visitors to the Southland . . ."

Freeth worked for several years as a sports trainer and lifeguard, but his career as the world's first professional surfer ended tragically. On April 7th, 1919, at age 35, this warm-blooded island boy died of a nasty influenza contracted after he had performed daring rescue work in the Oceanside area during a chilling winter storm.

Dr. John Heath Ball, more commonly referred to as "Doc" Ball, recalls in his folksy book, *California Surfriders* (1946), that Freeth early-on distinguished himself in California as a heroic figure. Ball recounts one Freeth adventure. It took place during the great Santa Monica Bay storm of December 16, 1908, when all by himself Freeth made "three freezing trips out through mountainous, foaming seas to rescue seven Japanese fishermen who were being swept to certain death in their small fishing boats."

For that brave deed, Ball reports, Freeth received kudos and public recognition awards. "And in addition," wrote Ball, "the populace of the fishing village near Port Angeles named their town 'Freeth' in his honor." He was indeed an important transitional character in the history of modern surfing, but as Ball has written, "too little is known today about this great and colorful figure . . ."

Duke Kahanamoku took up where Freeth left off, and the surfing devotees of these two swimming Hawaiians carried the surfing bug from there. Techniques and equipment grew more and more refined, and by 1928 California's surfriders were so together that they announced, in half-page advertisements in *The Santa Ana Daily Register*, a first Pacific Coast Surf Board Championship meet. The public was invited to bring picnic

GEORGE FREETH
FIRST SURFER IN THE UNITED STATES

GEORGE FREETH WAS BORN IN HONOLULU NOVEMBER 8, 1883 OF ROYAL HAWAIIAN AND IRISH ANCESTRY. AS A YOUNGSTER HE REVIVED THE LOST POLYNESIAN ART OF SURFING WHILE STANDING ON A BOARD. HENRY E. HUNTINGTON WAS AMAZED AT FREETH'S SURFING AND SWIMMING ABILITIES AND INDUCED GEORGE TO COME TO REDONDO IN 1907 TO PROMOTE THE BUILDING OF "THE LARGEST SALTWATER PLUNGE IN THE WORLD."

GEORGE FREETH WAS ADVERTISED AS "THE MAN WHO CAN WALK ON WATER." THOUSANDS OF PEOPLE CAME HERE ON THE BIG RED CARS TO WATCH THIS ASTOUNDING FEAT. GEORGE WOULD MOUNT HIS BIG 8 FOOT-LONG, SOLID WOOD, 200-POUND SURFBOARD FAR OUT IN THE SURF, HE WOULD WAIT FOR A SUITABLE WAVE, CATCH IT, AND TO THE AMAZEMENT OF ALL, RIDE ON TO THE BEACH WHILE STANDING UPRIGHT.

GEORGE FREETH INTRODUCED THE GAME OF WATER POLO TO THIS COAST. HE TRAINED MANY CHAMPION SWIMMERS AND DIVERS. GEORGE WAS THE FIRST "OFFICIAL LIFE GUARD" ON THE PACIFIC COAST. HE INVENTED THE TORPEDO SHAPED RESCUE BUOY THAT IS NOW USED WORLD WIDE. ON DECEMBER 12, 1908, DURING A VIOLENT SOUTH BAY STORM, GEORGE RESCUED 6 JAPANESE FISHERMEN FROM A CAPSIZED BOAT. FOR HIS VALOR HE RECEIVED "THE UNITED STATES LIFE SAVING CORPS GOLD MEDAL."

GEORGE FREETH DIED APRIL 7, 1919 AT THE EARLY AGE OF 35 YEARS AS THE RESULT OF EXHAUSTION FROM STRENUOUS RESCUE WORK.

baskets and enjoy, "absolutely free," demonstrations of surfboard riding by "world famous figures" such as Duke Kahanamoku of Hawaii, Tom Blake of Redondo, Gerrard and Art Vultee of the Los Angeles Athletic Club, Clyde Swedson (swimming coach of the Hollywood Athletic Club) and "other experts" such as L. Jarvis, R. Williams and H. Hutchinson.

"In addition to surf board races there will be canoe tilting contests, paddling races and a surfboard life-saving demonstration. The event is being staged by the Corona Del Mar Surf Board Club, the largest club of this kind in America," said *The Daily Register* of July 31, 1928.

On that same sports page was a story about Brooklyn Dodgers pitching star "Dazzy" Vance, and an Old Gold cigarette advertisement which featured New York Yankees superstar Lou Gehrig participating in a blindfolded cigarette smoking test. Gehrig, in Yankee pinstripes, is shown test-puffing four different cigarettes and concluding that "Old Gold has the most on the ball." That advertisement, improbably placed below a headline that said "Kahanamoku to Ride Surf at Harbor Sunday," was a sign of the times.

On the day of the big surfing contest, August 5, 1928, the largest crowd "that has visited the beach in the last five years" witnessed the first surf board races ever staged in Southern California.

It was at this premier West Coast meet that swimmer-surfer Tom Blake introduced his recently invented "Hawaiian Hollow Surfboard." Blake and his new board were very nearly laughed off the beach when he first put it on public display. However, he won that day's grueling paddling competition handily and — more important — mightily impressed previously skeptical California surfriders.

Blake was on to something, and during the next few years almost every surfer on the coast be-gan turning in their old spruce pine and redwood planks for lighter, Blake-style paddleboards. "The trend [in surfing] soon changed, due to its [the hollow board's] extreme lightness, strength, durability and the greater ease in gaining speed, with much less effort," a surfside analyst of the late 1930s noted.

Delbert "Bud" Higgins, a Huntington Beach lifeguard of those times, recently told *Los Angeles Times* reporter Jack Boettner that "the redwoods were really too heavy, about 125 pounds, plus another 10 pounds or so when they got wet." Yet, Higgins — who had the dubious distinction of having been the first man to ride through the pilings of the Huntington Beach Pier while standing on his head — also claimed that the old wooden boards were "so big and stable [that] you could do almost anything." *Santa Ana Register* reporter Stan Oftelie quotes him as saying:

"I remember one fella who used to bring a little folding camp stool and a parasol along with him when he'd paddle out. He'd catch a good wave, unfold the seat, then sit down and enjoy the ride in the shade."

The lighter "hollow board" revolutionized surfing by reducing the weight of a board from a "Roaring Twenties" average of 125 to 150 pounds to a mid-1930s mean of about 75 to 100 pounds. Steering and stability, however, were still a problem. Except for simple angle turn maneuvers, usually accomplished by dragging one's foot, Hawaiian-style, off a board's inside rail, or by stepping back and tilt-dancing the board around and out of its old track and into a new one, the new boards were still awkward and cumbersome. Once again, Blake offered a solution.

In 1935, Blake attached a simple fixed fin (now commonly called a skeg) to the bottom end of his patented paddleboard. That seemingly obvious innovation allowed a surfer to track and

The enlarged surf decal, left, appeared on a 1940 model of a paddleboard designed by surfing pioneer Tom Blake and built, improbably, by the Los Angeles Ladder Company.

pivot more freely, and gave the board more lateral stability. With such previously unexploited potentials for vicarious navigation, surfing's "fun factor" was once again amplified. The old Hawaiian-style surfing days of "dead ahead," "sliding ass," "all together now, turn," and "straight off, Adolph" were now absolutely *pau*. Finished, that is.

Such startling developments also made the sport *more* exciting for spectators. The Pacific Coast Surfriding Championship became an annual affair now, dominated for four out of the next eight years by the late Preston "Pete" Peterson of Santa Monica. Peterson reigned as California's top surfer during 1932, 1936, 1938, and 1941. Other early surfing champs included Keller Watson (1929), Gardner Lippincott (1934), Loren Harrison (1939) and Cliff Tucker (1940).

Tucker, the 1940 champion, says flat out that his former schoolmate and surfing pal, Peterson, "was the greatest waterman on the West Coast in those days. As far as I'm concerned, he was the best and maybe Loren Harrison was second best. I was hot one year and beat 'em both, but I was just lucky." Tucker was also clever.

During a recent interview from his home in Long Beach, Tucker recalled that in the early 1930s surfing days — "when a *man* could still be arrested at Santa Monica Beach for not wearing a top" — competition surfing was heavy-duty (equipment-wise) and tough (physically).

"If you were in a contest situation and a guy took off in front of you," he recalled, "it was your obligation to show no decency. You either went right through him or otherwise mowed him down." Tucker said that in the 1940 championship meet, held at San Onofre, "I won by switching boards at the proper times. I rode an 'ultralight,' a hollow, 50-pound plywood board, in the morning, and then when the chop came up later in the day, I switched to a heavier, 120-pound spruce.

Once enough people were eliminated, and I didn't need the extra weight for personal protection, I went back to the more maneuverable ultralight (known in surfing circles as a 'Slantwise'). In those days", Tucker notes, "I could build myself a spruce plywood 'ultralight' with about five dollars worth of materials."

Tucker, like many of California's early surf stars, was a member of the state's first and then most prestigious surf club, the Palos Verdes Surfing Club, whose members frequented the thick wave break off Palos Verdes' Bluff Cove. He remembers even earlier surfing times when he and Peterson, both classmates in the 6th grade, "would ditch school to go surfing" in waters near the old Crystal Pier Bathhouse at Santa Monica Beach. The Peterson family owned the bathhouse at that time.

"For years," Tucker said, "surfing was the biggest thing in my life. I remember thinking that if I couldn't ride a wave again, I couldn't live. I really thought that there was nothing else in the world that I'd rather do." Has he any regrets now? "I wish we had the equipment then that the kids have now. It's absolutely amazing what's being done on a surfboard these days. I'm sure we were just as strong and capable then as athletes, but we just didn't have the technology that's evolved in surfing since then."

Tucker's self-designed and self-built "Slantwise," also called a "Slantcher," was ultra-light and innovative for its time, but it wasn't until after World War II — at the beginning of the so-called technological boom era — that high surf tech came into its own.

During the war years, most of the beach boys who had hitherto spent their every bit of free time *on the blue* became, by Executive Order, *boys in blue*. Concertina wire was rolled onto the beaches in Hawaii and California, and surfing — a pastime

Members of the Palos Verdes Surf Club, left, mugged for this party time portrait in 1939 at their favorite after waves hangout, south Los Angeles' Zamboanga Bar, the renowned "home of the tailless monkies." At center is Cliff Tucker, the 1940 state surfing champ, and from left to right are Hal Landis, Art Rogers, Hal Pearson, Bob Johnson, Al Holland and Bernie Zeller

The Palos Verdes Surfing Club
Fourth Annual
HULA LUAU

El Portero Country Club
3410 West Manchester Boulevard

Saturday, March 16
9 P. M.
Sport $1.10

GET OUT OF THE
SOUP AND SLIDE

that was classified impractical and self-indulgent — entered into limbo. Between Pearl Harbor Day and VJ Day, no surfing contests were held. Many were the perfect, glassy waves that broke riderless on California's reefs, beaches, and points.

Joe Quigg, a Honolulu-based boatbuilder who is regarded by peers as one of contemporary surfing's most important craftsmen-innovators, recently recalled what the great surfing spot Malibu was like during the wartime summer of '44.

"I was in the Navy during the war, and I came home to Santa Monica on leave that year. Right after I got home, I drove up to Malibu to surf, and though the waves were good that day, there were only three guys out. One was a guy with a withered arm named Bob Simmons, and the other two were kids named Buzzy Trent and Matt Kivlin."

Simmons, Quigg learned later, had filled a void of sorts during the war years by building traditional surfboards for people who could still enjoy the sport. "To make money, he had started remodeling old-fashioned boards for people," Quigg said.

Following the war, in early 1946, Quigg was joined by a former Santa Monica High School classmate, Dave Rochlen, who was on a leave from the Marines. "Dave and I got curious about Simmons. We were still into surfing, and we heard he was building boards in his garage in Pasadena, so we drove over to see what he was up to." They found Simmons busy building three traditional redwood surfboards. "At that time he was still selling and talking up big, heavy boards, the same kind we'd always used," Quigg said.

Quigg recalls that he wasn't too impressed by Simmons at that time, but Rochlen said that "when we first met Simmons, we knew he was *different*. We knew he was somehow special, and we knew he was up to something. We called him a mad scientist."

Even at that early date, Simmons — "the only guy anybody could buy boards from during those years" — had already attracted a cult. One of his most avid sidekicks was Buzzy Trent, a big, husky kid who tagged along with Simmons on impromptu surfing safaris. They traveled in a souped up Model A Ford with its back end cut out to accommodate surfboards. "Together, they were a real pair — like the mad scientist and his big, burly sidekick Igor," says Rochlen.

At the time, Simmons was enrolled in courses at the nearby California Institute of Technology ("Not for credit, but for knowledge, he used to say," Rochlen remembers). His purpose was to learn all he could about aero and hydro dynamics. Following the war, Simmons began adapting some of the theories he'd learned at Cal Tech to surfboard-building and waveriding. He toyed with the first twin fin boards with concave bottoms, and, later, began experimenting with nose and tail contours and rounded rails. Some surfer-observers of that period say that Simmons was compelled to modify the shapes and weights of his surfboards because of his handicap. It was hard for him to use the heavy redwood and pine paddleboards then in vogue; he was constantly trying to make his one-armed surfing easier.

During 1949, Quigg says, Matt [Kivlin] began talking to Simmons about the idea of making lighter, hollow plywood rescue boards. "Simmons thought that was interesting, but instead of simply making the boards hollow he began sandwiching styrofoam between plywood and glassing the whole thing over. He had gotten some samples of styrofoam after the war, and had always dreamed of making a board with styrofoam." Styrofoam, however, would dissolve once catalyzed resin was poured onto it, so it was impractical. However, by sandwiching styrofoam between plywood, you could make it work.

A 'Hula Luau' ticket, left, publicized the 1940 dinner meeting of the active and partying Palos Verdes Surfing Club. The surfer is Cliff Tucker, as seen from the Hermosa Beach Pier.

The first such Simmons-made "Sandwich Boards" were simple affairs — plywood sealed over styrofoam. Later, he added light and shapeable balsa rails to streamline them.

"The lifeguards, unfortunately, never would buy them, but the surfers — Simmons' followers — thought they were neat and started buying them," said Quigg. Orders began piling up, and to satisfy the demand, Simmons set up a surf shop in Santa Monica. "In those first days, Simmons would glue the plywood, styrofoam and balsa parts together, then Matt [Kivlin] would shape the balsa rails and glass them over," said Quigg.

During the post-War years, Quigg left California to surf and live in Hawaii, but when Simmons' new board-building business became too big for him and Kivlin to handle by themselves, they asked Quigg to return to California and help them. Simmons maintained his original Santa Monica shop, and Quigg and Kivlin organized a separate glassing and finishing shop to support his operation. "Matt and I rented a shop space up the same road from Simmons' shop, and it was there that we did all the finishing work. At that time, Simmons had lots of orders. We did maybe a hundred boards," said Quigg.

Ideas were being popped out as fast as new surfboards, and during the late 1940s and early 1950s, Quigg, Kivlin and Simmons began carrying their board-building crafts into new realms. Quigg, as an example, fashioned surfing's first fiberglass fins during that period. All three began scooping up the noses of their boards, dropping the rails, and shaping the tailblocks in various experimental ways. Out of design sessions came innovations such as an early Simmons "Spoon" — a 10-foot solid male balsa (heavier than female balsa) board with a full belly, kicked up nose, thin rails and a glassed and foiled wooden fin — and a Quigg "Hot Curl" model *sans* fin.

Rochlen, then an L.A. County lifeguard, also began building boards, said Quigg. "I used to play around with tints to make the boards look a little bit different, but Dave was the first person I recall who began applying modern-style, colorful designs onto surfboards." Rochlen recalls fashioning custom boards for the actors Gary Cooper and Peter Lawford "and other movie industry people."

Quigg says that long before he and Simmons began experimenting with balsa and foam, there were always light redwood-balsa and balsa surfboards around. "In the early California and Hawaii surfing days they were considered beginners' or girls' boards," said Quigg. "The bigger and older waveriders wouldn't be seen on a light board, and when a kid or a girl would paddle out on one, they'd chase them away and make them surf on the smaller, inside waves.

"But during that time when Simmons' followers were switching over from old-fashioned redwoods to his new plywood and styrofoam models, I began to make a few really light 24-pound boards for my wife and some of her friends. For some reason, this got Simmons mad. He still had a thing about long and wide boards and couldn't understand why I wanted to make such *short* boards."

Quigg recalls that these 9-foot balsa boards, considered very small in those days, were a big hit with his wife and her girlfriends. "So Matt [Kivlin] bought some balsa from me and made his girlfriend a nice, streamlined nine-six board. That was Matt's first light, all-balsa board."

Out of curiosity, and apparently for fun, Quigg says, Kivlin began surfing on his girlfriend's smaller board. "And about the same time, another local surfer by the name of Leslie Williams began borrowing my wife's balsa board."

"In those days," he said, "Matt was the best surfer around, so he made quite an impression on

Tooling along on a little Palos Verdes Estate curl, left, is Jim Bailey and his famous surfing cocker spaniel named "Rusty." This "surf classic" was shot by early surf photographer John Heath "Doc" Ball.

113

A gallery of early
L.A. locals shout
encouragement from the
infamous "Pit" at Malibu.
This fascinating
snapshot was clicked
during the "uncrowded"
summer of 1953.

people who saw him on that light board. And Williams, he *really* got into my wife's board. He started doing things nobody had ever seen before. He was the first guy I knew of who made radical bank turns. He would lay out on a wave and just generally rip. Together, Kivlin and Williams made quite a splash and began setting the style for everybody who was watching them.

"What they did, as far as I'm concerned, busted the whole surfing thing right open. When other surfers saw what Matt and Leslie were doing, it was the beginning of the end for old-fashioned and crude surfing. After that, no hot surfer ever built an old redwood or paddleboard again. And surfing left its 'crude' period."

Also nearing an end was surfing's so-called "Simmons Era." For all his apparent genius, Simmons could not do anything about his physical limitations, and eventually, after many seasons of teasing the sea, he died in her waves.

On the afternoon of September 26, 1954, Robert Wilson Simmons, 35, of a Pasadena, California, Oakland Street address, was reported missing in big surf and dangerous riptides off San Diego's Windansea surfing beach. Three days later, his body was found at the foot of Bonair Street at the north end of Windansea. Ironically, that spot is now the favored hangout of La Jolla-area surfers and the site of Windansea's famed Polynesian thatch hut and "surfers' parking lot."

Unfortunately, Simmons did not live to see the new era, four years later, when easier-to-work-with polyurethane foam became commercially available to the surfboard-building industry. What could he have wrought with such tools? In his stead were contemporaries Kivlin, Quigg, and newly emerging craftsmen such as Dale Velzy, Hap Jacobs and Dewey Weber of Hermosa Beach, Reynolds Yater of Santa Barbara, Dave Sweet of Santa Monica, and the most enterprising boardbuilder of them all,

Hobie Alter, then of artsy Laguna Beach.

Quigg says that for years he tried to find better, more durable board-building materials, but it wasn't until 1958 that a Los Angeles-area company — the American Latex Company — began making polyurethane blanks that were durable enough for surfboards. "Dave Sweet, Gordon Clark, Hobie and I all seemed to find out about the stuff at the same time, and we all started making boards with it. I have no idea who bought it first, but there must be a purchase order over there (at the American Latex Company) that could tell you."

Another surfing phenomenon that greatly influenced the direction surfing began to take during the late Forties and early Fifties was a sort of cross-pollination of styles and equipment theories that began taking place between Hawaii and California. Far away Australia was developing a mutant surfing culture all its own, and its day in surfing's sun would yet dawn, but most progressive theories and equipment of those post-War times were being tested and perfected in and around California and Hawaii surf spots.

Surfing contests were resumed in California and Hawaii after World War II, but, as before, the highlight of such competitions was more often than not a grueling and then traditional paddling race. From 1948 to 1952, for example, the star in California surfing circles was Tom Zahn, yet another classmate at Santa Monica High of Quigg-Rochlen-et al. Zahn, like some other surf pilgrims, eventually ended up in Hawaii, where, as early as 1953, he distinguished himself by paddling a racing board through the 36 miles of rough seas between the islands of Molokai and Oahu.

Hawaii's west and north shores in the winter are generally acknowledged to be the sites of "the best waves in the world." By 1954, the year of the first Makaha International Surfing Championships, small bands of California surfers had be-

gun making an annual trek to Hawaii. *Honolulu Star-Bulletin* reporter Sarah Park reported on January 7 of that year:

> If you asked the average Islander to point out Makaha to you, you'd probably run into a lot of inaccurate pointing . . . But a small band of Californians have found Makaha without any trouble. They are content to go without the usual luxuries of modern day living, just so they can surf there. Three Californians arrived about 10 days ago to join a hardy band of some 15 ascetics living in a shack about two blocks from the surf. The new arrivals have taken a cottage across the street — for $10 a month each — and have scattered swim fins, spears, and surfboards around their new house-with-kitchen — the kitchen being a Coleman stove.

Miss Park went on to describe this peculiar surfer lifestyle evolving on Oahu's leeward side. "Overhead, surfboards hang by rope so they can be let down with ease, while swim fins hang on chairs scattered in between seven beds, bunks and cots." A photograph captioned "From California to Makaha" showed this group of mainland surfers. Among them were Buzzy Trent and California buddies Philip "Flippy" Hoffman, Chuck McClelland, Junior Knox, Jim Fisher and Ted Crane. Said Trent to reporter Park: "We have a garden, we spear our fish — yesterday Junior Knox got us a 65-pound turtle — and we have salads, stews and things. It's a community thing. We are over here strictly to surf, and corny as it may sound, the surf over here is terrific. It's the best."

In a sort of mutual exchange, meanwhile, Hawaiian surfers such as George Downing, Woody Brown and Wally Froiseth began making visits to California to check out that *country's* waves. Steve Pezman, an early California to Hawaii surfari-ist who now serves as publisher of *Surfer* magazine, recalled in a special 1983 "Surfer Style" issue of his publication how such California-Hawaii relationships — and styles — evolved during this important period in surfing history:

> In the postwar late 1940s George Downing and a couple of fellow Waikiki beach boys crewed a sailboat back to California and surf-cruised the coast. They tasted Malibu as we had tasted Castles surf. And in the early 50's another group of California surfers, including Burrhead and Walter Hoffman, joined with George and some of the Waikiki crew in exploring Makaha. The Californians camped on the beach at Makaha and quickly adopted the island style of living. They were treated to the aloha spirit and were much in awe of their Hawaiian watermen friends and their wonderful islands.
> In turn, the Hawaiian surfers had warm feelings for these few Californians who seemed so eager to learn their ways and who exhibited great skill and courage in the surf. Together they shared profound moments of discovery about what could be done on these majestic waves and how much a man could endure and overcome. They rode together with grace and control in warm violent seas that dwarfed those men but not their spirits.
> These early pioneers who traveled to Hawaii brought back to the mainland certain symbols of the warm aloha of Hawaii. They wore the flowered print silk shirts of the islands, casual, colorful, loose and easy. And the thong slaps. And the classic surfer shorts, cut longer to just above the knee to protect the leg from rubbing on the waxed

A smiling trio of young surfing Californians bid Hawaii aloha in the 1952 portrait at left. Under the coconut hats are, from left, Joe Quigg, Matt Kivlin and Tom Zahn, all of faraway Santa Monica.

California surf masters
Tom Zahn (left) and Joe
Quigg show off their
Malibu Perpetual
Surfboard trophy during
a 1951 wave break.

deck. With a lace closure that could be firmly cinched to keep from being rudely removed by the waves. At Windansea Beach and San Onofre grass shacks were built, not unlike the palapas on the beach at Waikiki . . .

Also during this time, West Coast kids began to get more and more involved in surfing. The newer, lighter surfboards brought the sport within range of nearly any family's pocketbook, so the chances of having a surfboard of one's own were not, as before, dictated by economic well-being. Boardbuilder Quigg credits a fellow craftsman, Dale Velzy, with "turning California's kids — his 'gremmies' he called them — on to surfing in a big way." Velzy joined forces with fellow Hermosa Beach waterman Harold "Hap" Jacobs in early 1953 and rented a little shop space just up the street from the Hermosa Beach Pier. There, they began custom-building boards under the Velzy-Jacobs imprint.

"What Velzy did, all along the Strand, from Hermosa to Manhattan and Redondo, was get all the little kids who wanted to surf onto his small boards. He got children 12 years and older out into the big breaks for the first time. These tiny kids were, well, tiny, so Velzy inadvertently made a lot of the first really small boards. But by doing so he really popularized the sport. He was really smart, Velzy. He was the first guy to sponsor surfers, the first guy to advertise in a big way, and the first guy to put surfboards — and thus surfing — within the reach of the average kid on the beach. Yeah, if you ask me, it was Velzy and his gremmies who started the whole mass surfing phenomena thing in California."

By the end of the 1950s, Velzy and Jacobs had separated and gone their own stylistic and business ways. And by 1960, when Velzy alone had three shops cranking out surfboards — at

Venice, San Clemente and San Diego — he was advertising himself as "The World's Largest Manufacturer."

Meanwhile, down south, the "big guys," as Quigg describes them, had begun buying their custom-made surfboards from a young and very enterprising boardbuilder named Hobart "Hobie" Alter. Quigg recalls that "those of us from up north used to go down south to show off our new equipment, usually at San Onofre, and a lot of people down there, including Hobie, became very interested in what we were up to." Alter, who grew up in the inland California town of Ontario, used to summer in a family home at Laguna Beach, that chic, seaside artists' colony about halfway between Corona Del Mar and San Onofre. He was not unlike most Southern Californians who became entranced by the summer sea and waveriding, but Alter did more than "just surf."

In a September, 1981, interview with Laura Bly of *The Santa Ana Daily Register*, Alter recalls that he first became a surfboard-building entrepreneur during high school days when he began building handmade surfboards in his father's Laguna Beach garage.

"I started out making maybe 20 boards a summer for my friends, and it sure beat being a lifeguard," Alter told Bly. "About the end of junior college — which took me a little longer because I was doing a lot of surfing and skiing — my father decided I'd learned everything I could, and he recommended I go into the board business full time."

With the advent of the aforementioned polyurethane foam, a durable but lightweight, waterproof plastic material, and easy-to-use fiberglassing materials, Hobie's backyard and garage hobby had become a commercially profitable pastime. With the backing of his financier-father, Alter in 1958 established a major surfboard-building shop and showroom in the south Orange

County beach town of Dana Point. Today, thousands of foam boards later, Alter has made his fortune — not just from surfboard sales, but also from the development and marketing of innovative skateboards, catamarans (Hobie Cats) and, most recently, a sleek new Hobie 33-foot mono-hull sloop that can be sailed singlehandedly and trailered from port to port.

Alter's early success, however, rode on foam, fiberglass and the advances in surf board design made possible by those technological factors. With such malleable materials, he — and his chemist-supplier, Gordon "Grubby" Clark — were able to sculpt popular "Malibu" boards of the time into even more aesthetic and functional wave-riding devices. No longer did they and others have to rely on weighty hardwoods and costly balsa.

When Alter began developing his first big Dana Point shop in 1958, one of the first shapers he hired was quiet-spoken Quigg.

"Hobie came to Hawaii, where I was once again living, told me he had orders for about 500 of the new foam boards, and said he needed my help," says Quigg. So yet again — as he had done when Simmons and Kivlin summoned him in 1949 — Quigg returned to California to build boards — this time for Hobie. "I couldn't believe the business he had. Sometimes I was shaping ten boards a day," Quigg recalls. Hobie, meanwhile, never looked back and went on to become one of surfing's — and now sailing's — most inventive and envied entrepreneurs.

Nobody knows when or why it happened, but sometime in the mid-1950s, Hollywood "discovered" surfing, and when that happened, this once semi-exclusive cult was jettisoned into a state of mass consciousness that no one could have dreamed would happen. This unexpected development was both a bane and a blessing, depending on one's philosophical point of view.

Preceding pages, a Sixties woodie still life, "Decals In Excess," by Jim Evans.

123

THE SIXTIES: 'SURFING U.S.A.'

During the summer of '56, about the time polyurethane foam first began making waves, a curious teenage "beach bunny" named Kathy Kohner started hanging out at Malibu. Day after sunny day she splashed in the 'Bu's shorebreak and marveled at the zany characters — "Tubesteak," "Moondoggie," "Pink" and other locals — who had adopted Malibu as their surfing home. Like many another California girl, Kathy wanted to be a "surfer girl."

After a few dues-paying summers, Malibu's resident hotdoggers allowed little Kathy into their inner circle. They took her out tandem surfing, regaled her with surf stories, and even gave her a proper surfer's nickname. Kathy, now a fortyish Pacific Palisades bookstore clerk named Kathy Zuckerman, recalled in a 1981 interview with *New West* magazine that the surfer "Tubesteak" christened her "Gidget" — short for "girl midget" — because she was only five feet tall.

In the evenings, after Kathy had returned home from daytime surfing adventures, she'd tell her family about her kookie Malibu friends and her role as the surfer girl named Gidget. Her father, Frederick "Fritz" Kohner, an author, found his daughter's stories fascinating, so he sat down at his typewriter and whipped out a novel, *Gidget*, based on Kathy's beach experiences. Kohner's effort — a first person narrative by Gidget, "the little girl with big ideas" — was a best-selling success, and shortly thereafter he and Putnam Books sold the movie rights to *Gidget* to Columbia Pictures.

With the highly-publicized screening of a first *Gidget* movie (1959), featuring chirp-chirp Sandra Dee in a frilly title role opposite teen heartthrob James Darren, America's then preponderant youth culture — of greasy hair, pegger pants and obliquely "raked" cars — got its first look at Southern California's sun-bleached surfing cult. Also, and some say unfortunately, the noble Hawaiian sport of surfing entered its most commer-cially successful, but cornball, era.

That first cutesy Gidget movie was such a success it spawned successor flicks — *Gidget Goes Hawaiian* (1961) and *Gidget Goes to Rome* (1963) — and a shortlived (1965–1966) ABC television series. Later Gidgets, *Gidget Grows Up* (1970) and *Gidget Gets Married* (1972), fidgeted their way into America's living rooms as television "Specials," but it was Kohner's novel, and Columbia's first two pastel and cream romances, that gave worlds beyond California and Hawaii their first distorted view of surfing.

Except for a few Malibu regulars who made bucks off Gidget mania as surfing extras (folks such as Mickey "Da Cat" Dora and Johnny "Bottom Turn" Fain), most Southern California surfers cringed when the movies premiered and they saw how their sport was interpreted by filmmakers. The Gidget films were undeniably geeky, but Gollywood was onto a favorite chase — a hypable and marketable trend — so during the next ten years the public was assaulted by so-called "beach movies" with bizarre and kitschy surfing themes. Vying for audience appeal during that decade were strange cinema clones such as *The Beach Girls and the Monster* (American Academy Productions, 1965) and *How to Stuff a Wild Bikini* (American International Pictures, 1965).

Surfers and non-surfers now laugh at the almost nauseating naivete of those early beach movies, but Hollywood producers remember them as commercial monsters — that is, as great money-makers. *Beach Party*, the trend-setting 1963 American International Pictures (A.I.P.) movie that cast teen idols Frankie Avalon and Annette Funicello as young surfers in love, set box-office records nationwide soon after its release. The spectre of these pasty and dark-haired Italian-Americans (singer Avalon and Mouseketeer Funicello) cast as Southern California surfers was

True to hotdog form, California surfer Mickey Munõz executes a picture perfect "quasimodo" pose.

ridiculous, but the movie quickly grossed some $3.5 million, a tidy sum in those days. That "youth market" winner was hastily followed by three other A.I.P. potboilers — *Muscle Beach Party* (1964), *Bikini Beach* (1964) and *Beach Blanket Bingo* (1965).

The plots woven into those early Hollywood "surfing movies" were unbearably thin. In *Beach Blanket Bingo,* for example, Frankie (Avalon), Dee Dee (Funicello) and fellow Hollywood surfers found themselves in yet another party-crashing confrontation with Eric Von Zipper (Harvey Lembeck) and his notorious motorcycle gang, the Rat Pack. Yes, fans, West Coast Story, or, as one will fondly recall, a Greasers versus Surfers stand off. Meanwhile, somewhere between a lame watusi dancing scene and stand-up shticks by Don "Big Drop" Rickles, Buster Keaton and Earl Wilson (as themselves), one of the surfers, Bonehead, is rescued from drowning by a beautiful mermaid named Lorelei (portrayed by Marta Kristen). It was high surfside camp at its best (or worst?).

As such surfing-related themes began to appeal to the mass consciousness, several other L.A. production companies began spewing out beach movies. Hollywood's scriptwriters gazed out of their Malibu Colony bungalows, rolled paper into their salt sprayed typewriters, and surged into second surfing gear.

Remember *Don't Make Waves* (Filmways, Inc. and Reynard Productions, 1967), that steamy little surf epic starring Tony Curtis, Claudia Cardinale and the late Sharon Tate? In that zinger the sultry Miss Tate portrays a surfer-skydiver (Malibu) who saves a visiting tourist (Carlo Cofield, played by Curtis) from drowning off Malibu Beach. The Tate-Curtis mouth-to-mouth resuscitation scene is a classic in surfing heroism. The movie is saved, however, by its theme song, "Don't Make Waves," written and performed by Chris Hillman and Jim

At the Redondo Breakwater, ca. 1961. This fine Sixties surfing moment was captured by Art Rogers of The Los Angeles Times. *Note the vintage narrow white Levis and Pendleton jackets worn by members of this stoked breakwater gallery.*

Mickey "Da Cat" Dora hangs a neat five on a perfect little wave at Malibu. Dora, probably more than any other surfer, established a sense of hotdogging cool that is still copied by young California surfers.

McGuinn of the then fledgling Byrds.

As has been true of many teenybopper genre movies since, it was the "background music" that usually saved the beach blanket movies and made them worth their then $1.50 admission price. *Beach Party,* as an example, marked the first nationwide appearance of Dick Dale (The "King of the Surf Guitar") and his reverb-ridden Del Tones. Some sound track debuts, though historically important, went virtually unnoticed. In small print at the bottom of a poster advertising *Muscle Beach Party* is a small credit line "Introducing Little Stevie Wonder." In yet another musical adventure — Paramount Pictures' *Beach Ball* (1965), starring Edd "Kookie" Byrnes of "77 Sunset Strip" television fame — bikinis coexisted with guest star appearances by The Supremes, The Four Seasons, The Righteous Brothers, the Walker Brothers and The Hondells. "Nothing Bounces Like 'Beach Ball'," proclaimed a period press release. "They're Surf Ridin' . . . Skin Divin' . . . Sky Jumpin' . . . Drag Racin' . . . Beach Bashin' Boys and their Bikini Beauties . . . in a Blast of a Beach Brawl!"

In December of 1964, a *New York Times* film critic, Peter Bart, traveled west, observed the making of a California beach blanket movie at Leo Carrillo Beach, and reported that this mutant cinematic form "has created a rather idyllic way of life for the young people who are regulars in the beach pictures.

"Most were members of the teen-age surfing set around Santa Monica before being 'discovered' by American International. They are thus living out a bizarre adolescent fantasy — making a great deal of money without ever leaving their beloved surfboards," Bart wrote. "The various members of the beach set," he added, "have grown so accustomed to their moviemaking routines that they can grind out a new 'beacher' in less than three weeks."

This Leroy Grannis photo of Johnny Fain leaning into a clean bottom turn at Malibu was for many years one of surfing's most coveted poster images. Two decades have passed since "Granny" took this flick, but on a good day at Malibu, you'll still see Fain out there surfing through today's young, "slash and burn" surf rats.

Perhaps the most archetypal and ambitious of those beach blanket wonders was Columbia Pictures' *Ride the Wild Surf* (1964), starring "Turn Me Loose" pop singing star Fabian Forte as big wave rider Jody Wallis. Also cast into this cinematic backwater were blonde heart breaker Tab Hunter (as the surfer "Steamer Lane") and pop star Shelley Fabares (as the foxy surfer girl Brie Matthews). Splashing about in supporting roles were Barbara Eden (as Augie Poole), Peter Brown (as Chase Colton), Susan Hart (as Lily Kilua), and James Mitchum (as the surfer "Eskimo").

A promotion for the movie — "Actually filmed in the 'wild waters' of Hawaii!" — explained that Steamer, Jody and Chase had "come to Oahu Island to ride the world's biggest waves and compete against surfers from all over the world. Steamer Lane falls in love with Lily Kilua, whose mother objects to the romance because she considers surfers to be 'beach bums' . . ."

In a particularly memorable scene, Chase generates monster waves at a flat Waimea Bay by diving into a pool beneath nearby Waimea Falls. According to a Columbia Pictures press release, Chase was invoking an ancient Hawaiian legend that says "if big waves fail to come in at Waimea Bay, a dive into the pool by one of the surfers will start the waves coming . . ." At triumphant moments in the movie, new Liberty Records singing stars Jan and Dean sing the movie's title song, "Ride the Wild Surf," written by Jan Berry (of Jan and Dean), Brian Wilson (chief songwriter for another new group, The Beach Boys) and Roger Christian.

In an attempt to give surfing a sportive credibility, Columbia Pictures promoted the film with testimonials from former collegiate and pro football star Frank Gifford. "See the spills and thrills the champ surfers take in *Ride the Wild Surf.* It packs as big a wallop as anything I've ever run across on the football field!" blurted Gifford in national radio, television and telephone publicity spots.

All the razzle-dazzle above marked a strange time in surfing history, but during that same carefree period — as the Greasy Fifties segued into the Sunny Sixties — true surfers remained hundreds of mind miles away from the glitter and dreck of Hollywood. Throughout and despite all that big screen embarrassment, California's surfing society continued to develop a character all its own. It evolved into an aloof cult that produced its own movies and music, discovered and annointed its own heroes, communicated intelligence about the surfing life in its own idiomatic way, and established a sense of "surfer style" and ritual that endures to this day.

The leading purveyor of surfing news and myths during this important evolutionary period was an ingenuous new publication called *The Surfer.* When *The Surfer* debuted in 1960 as a black and white booklet with a two-color cover, it was simply meant to be a nice, salable brochure to help promote surf movies being made by John Severson, an enterprising Capistrano High School art instructor. However, because it filled a yawning need as the first ideas forum published by and for surfers, *The Surfer* was well received. Indeed, its first issue's success was so heartening that school teacher-filmmaker Severson left his classroom to become surfing's first publisher-editor.

In *The Surfer,* which later shortened its name to *Surfer,* surfers could talk to and hear from fellow waveriders. They could test float radical new equipment ideas, go on vicarious worldwide surfaris with *Surfer's* colorful team of writers, artists and photographers, and marvel at the latest in secret surfing spots. I mean, really brah, where else could Stinson or Ocean Beach locals learn about hydroplane board designs being wave-tested in

THE SURFER

Hawaii? Or read in-depth about last month's Bell's Beach Surf Classic? Or discover that on a good day you can ride from France into Spain on a wave that curls across the mouth of the border river La Bidassoa?

Publisher Severson started his magazine with only $3,000 and lots of fun, surf-related ideas. A decade later, *Surfer* was a slick monthly with a paid circulation of nearly 100,000. In 1970 *The Los Angeles Times* called *Surfer* magazine "the only magazine of national consequence published in Orange County."

In Orange County? Though this amorphous administrative region between Los Angeles and San Diego is more well known for its right wing Republicanism and Disneyland, it has also evolved into an important surfing place. Both historically and politically it is renowned in contemporary surfing power circles as "the unofficial surfing capital of the world."

Elliott Almond, who regularly writes fine surfing-related stories for the Orange County and regular editions of *The Los Angeles Times*, notes: "There may be bigger and more spectacular waves in Mexico, Hawaii, Australia and Indonesia, but the evolution — and sometimes revolution — the sport has undergone through the years has, for the most part, been rooted among Orange County's surfers."

Almond's home county bias is well founded. He points out, among other things, that Orange County is *the* editorial headquarters (at Capistrano) of surfing's two most important publications, *Surfer* and *Surfing;* that the sport's two most successful and influential filmmakers, Bruce Brown (*The Endless Summer*) and Greg MacGillivray (*Five Summer Stories*) live there (at Dana Point and South Laguna); and that Gordon "Grubby" Clark, long the world's leading manufacturer of foam board blanks, and Hobie Alter, surf-

ing's first commercially successful board-maker, both got their starts in and have remained in the county (in the San Clemente-Dana Point area). Also based in Orange County are surfwear manufacturers Walter and Philip "Flippy" Hoffman and surfing's greatest 1960s "star," Phil Edwards. Because these influential businessmen-surfers were traditionally headquartered on or near Beach Road in the San Clemente-Dana Point area, they became known to other people in the surfing trade as the "Dana Point Mafia." According to popular myth, this group of good ol' beachboys has the commercial surfing world sewn tightly into its money-filled wax pockets.

Norman B. Chandler, another surfing *L.A. Times*-man, wrote in 1980 of this south Orange County clan: "All are friends of more than 25 years. All were among the first surfers in this country. All have beach-houses next to each other worth up to a million dollars each." But most important, Chandler notes, "they also comprise a successful group of businessmen who are leaders in exporting various components of beach living." They were the Southern California dream image personified — tanned, straw-haired, successful, and always following the sun.

All of the above surfioso were caught up in a commercial surfing swell that hit California's shores in the late 1950s. But unlike many who wiped out — or burned out — early on, they rode this surfy trend to personal success. "They all recognized some magical ingredient in the Southern California lifestyle, took a part of it, and made it their own," recalls Steve Pezman, who later succeeded Severson as the publisher of *Surfer* magazine.

These Dana Point types may have indeed been a cliquish lot, but they took their sport — and business — seriously, and in the end contributed a much-needed sense of stability and credibility to surfing.

The fuzzy, but important big wave picture at left appeared on this cover of the first issue of The Surfer *magazine that was written, photographed and published by then surf filmmaker John Severson. Taking a drop at Hawaii's awesome Sunset Beach surf spot is a late big wave master, Jose Angel.*

Posing for a 1964 group portrait are, at right, members of the prestigious Windansea Surf Club. Many of these smiling surfers were or went on to become regional, national and international surfing stars.

*Words and music by Brian Wilson, copyright ©1963 by Irving Music, Inc. (BMI). International copyright secured. All rights reserved. Used by permission.

Just get away from the shady turf,
And baby catch some rays on the sunny surf.
And when you catch a wave,
You'll be sitting on top of the world.
— lyrics from Catch A Wave, 1963,
by Brian Wilson of the Beach Boys*

1963: It was the Southern California summer of our content. Behind the pitching of Sandy Koufax, Don Drysdale and Johnny Podres, the Los Angeles Dodgers were the all-time greatest team in baseball. Kookie had quit lending people his comb. Martin Luther King had a dream. And our favorite President, Kennedy, was still alive, smiling and saying "this about that."

It was also a great summer for waves. Ab, Newbreak and San Miguel were relatively undiscovered and pumping. "Killer Dana" and Doheny had not yet been paved over. Classical Malibu was flawless. And the Mac Meda Destruction Company was hosting outrageous parties near La Jolla's infamous Pump House.

Yes, Gidget, Frankie and Annette were a drag (definitely not bitchen or boss), but surfing's hard core — those who knew — ignored such kooks and hodads anyway. The true surfiati were at the Santa Monica Civic Auditorium hooting at real surf movies — flicks such as Bruce Brown's Surfing Hollow Days, John Severson's Surf Classics and Bob Evans' The Young Wave Hunters. Or they were moving up and down in the tribal motions of the "surfer's stomp" at dance venues of the time — places like the Rendezvous Ballroom in Balboa, Harmony Park (off the freeway in Anaheim) and even "inland" at Riverside's cavernous National Guard Armory.

Outside, in the parking lot, woodies and Nomads were stuffed full of surfboards and sleeping bags; inside, seminal surf groups — such as the Chantays, Surfaris and Dick Dale and the Del

Tones — let their tremolos and reverbs run wild. Pendleton wools, bleeding Madras cottons, white Levis, surf shop T-shirts (Remember the Wardy, Ole and Con logos?), huarache sandals and black Converse All-Star tennis shoes rose and stomped through anthems such as "Pipeline," "Wipeout," "Miserlou" and "Let's Go Trippin'."

Dick Dale, who since early 1961 had been the reigning "King of the Surf Guitar," pranced and posed as a surfer, but his swarthy, jelly roll looks were, ironically, more pomade than peroxide. Dale, a native of Boston, was a mutation showcast somewhere between Frank Zappa, Fabian and the glitter-shirted regulars who frequented car club dances at the El Monte Legion Stadium (where cats and chicks were invited to "meet old friends and make new friends, but no jeans or capris, please"). His was a strange evolution, but whatever his anthropomorphic or social bent, Dale and his Del Tones packed Southern California ballrooms and armories weekend after weekend during more than three years of exciting surf music nights. Throughout those early Sixties times, when the now nearly institutionalized Beach Boys were still lip-synching to 45 rpm records at summer YMCA "sock hops," King Dale was playing to audiences of at least 3,000 to 4,000-plus, three and four nights a week.

Like rock and roll generally, "surf music" was greatly influenced by the then quickly changing moods of rockabilly and rhythm and blues. Transition artists such as Chuck Berry, Duane Eddy and the inventive oldtimer, Les Paul, had long been experimenting with tremolos, echolettes and other such techno music toys, but these gimmicks were usually utilized for the odd temporary effect. Not until Dale began promoting himself as a surf guitarist, and calling such sustained electro riffs "surf music," was this peculiar sound given a popular or proper generic name. Early Dale sin-

gles, notably "Let's Go Trippin'," "Miserlou" and "Death of a Gremmie," began a slow but sure climb up pop record charts.

With left-handed and upside-down guitarist Dale leading the way, instrumental surf bands — not unlike New Wave/Punk bands today — began emerging from every other suburban tract home garage. And not just in Southern California. Formidable "inland" surf groups — such as The Trashmen (Remember their dorky single, "Surfing' Bird"?) from Minneapolis, the Astronauts from mile-high Denver, and The "Walk-Don't Run" Ventures of non-sunny Seattle — adopted the surfing sound and reverberated their way into California's — and the country's — Top Ten.

About that same twangy time, the Beach Boys — a harmonious quintet from the South Bay town of Hawthorne — and a loosely-related second group — Jan and Dean — injected yet another element into surfing and music. Their contribution was mixed harmonies and documentary (some say poetic) lyrical treatments. Unlike Dale and guitar-slashing others who imitated the sounds and feelings of surfing instrumentally, the Beach Boys and Jan and Dean communicated what they felt about surfing — and Southern California's youth culture — by singing about it in lilting two, three or four part harmony. Their choral stuff was simple, a la the Four Freshmen, but pretty, catchy and, most important, relevant to the times. Cars, waves, and girls were "happening" in Southern California then, and these two groups interpreted that adolescent era perfectly.

Indeed, when the Beach Boys advised us that everybody was "goin' surfin', surfin' U.S.A.," and Jan (Berry) and Dean (Torrance) assured us that in Surf City there would be "two girls for every boy," we believed their every word. We "War Babies" were more than ready. We waxed down our surfboards, couldn't wait till June, and from San Ono-

fre to Sunset we prepared to cruise Colorado Boulevard in little deuce coupes and 409s. Fast cars — and tasty waves — were there for the taking — if we stayed away from "Dead Man's Curve."

Probably the most influential "character" and spokesman for this particular musical age was Brian Wilson, the reclusive Beach Boy who wrote many of the most memorable lyrics for the Beach Boys and Jan and Dean. Wilson was probably most effective because he wrote of what he knew best. From his room in the Wilson home on the corner of Hawthorne Boulevard and 119th Street, Brian composed some of surfing's — and popular culture's — most successful and hummable musical standards.

In a summer of '83 tribute to Southern California's Beach Boys — to mark the fact that the boys had been invited by President Reagan to sing at the White House — *Los Angeles Times* reporter Paul Feldman recalled the following fascinating Brian Wilson story:

It was about 1960 that Brian, now 40, but then a student at Hawthorne High School, began composing the tunes that were to make the group famous . . . Then, however, his music was not universally popular. Fred Morgan, the high school band director, recalled flunking Brian in music composition for writing "a song with a bunch of chords in it" rather than the sonata he'd requested. "I gave him an F on a composition that later became known as 'Surfin' U.S.A.'" Morgan said.

Yes, '63 really was a fine year. Drastic change was in the air, but America's seemingly invincible youth were swept up in an exciting and "free" era punctuated by drugs, sex, rock 'n roll and politics. Socially, most young people were sitting on a strange cusp — somewhere between a frat-rat/

jock alcohol-based consciousness and the first stirrings of psychedelia, hippie-ness and what law enforcement officials liked to call "a false sense of euphoria." All the above predated an unpopular war in Vietnam, and nobody in this generation could imagine — or care — what words like "inflation," "recession" and "oil cartel" would mean two decades later. In 1963, petrol cost 19 to 29 cents a gallon at the neighborhood U-Save, so for five dollars split four ways you could check out every surf spot along a good 100 mile stretch of Pacific Coast Highway.

Surf music, the stomp and related surf-related manias hung in there strong until about the mid-Sixties when they were superseded by influential and new cultural waves. Notable were the aforementioned drugs and war in Vietnam, but more profound was a curious form of Brittanic rock and roll being exported to America by a mop-topped quartet from England called The Beatles. The effects of this stoney "British Invasion" were so profound that once glamorous surfers soon found themselves floating quietly in a cultural backwater. The late Jimi Hendrix, a young Seattle guitarist who had migrated to England, and who like Dick Dale played his Fender Stratocaster left-handed and upside down, was heard mumbling ominously (in a popular, screeching song, "Third Stone From The Sun") that "you'll never hear surf music again." Jimi was not entirely right, but he did realize that something was amiss.

But despite such portents of doom, surfing once again surged into the mass consciousness. During the chaotic summer of 1964, when all seemed to be going goofy in Surf City and the world, a mild-mannered Southern California film-maker named Bruce Brown premiered a rough, "budget" surfing movie, *The Endless Summer*, that inadvertently catapulted surfing into its longest and most influential public relations ride ever.

The Endless Summer

On any day of the year it's summer somewhere in the world. Bruce Brown's latest color film highlights the adventures of two young American surfers, Robert August and Mike Hynson who follow this everlasting summer around the world. Their unique expedition takes them to Senegal, Ghana, Nigeria, South Africa, Australia, New Zealand, Tahiti, Hawaii and California. Share their experiences as they search the world for that perfect wave which may be forming just over the next Horizon. **BRUCE BROWN FILMS**

Bruce Brown Films the producer of "Slippery When Wet," "Surf Crazy," "Barefoot Adventure," "Surfing Hollow Days," "Waterlogged" and "The Endless Summer."

KILGORE
I can take that point and hold it just as long
as I like, and you can get any place up that
river that suits you, young Captain. Hell, a
six foot peak. All right, take a gunship back
to the division. Lance, go with Mike and let
him pick out a board for you and bring me
my Yater Spoon, the eight six.

MIKE
I don't know sir, it's ah . . .

KILGORE
What is it soldier?

MIKE
Well, I mean it's pretty hairy in there, it's,
it's Charlie's Point.

KILGORE
Charlie don't surf.

Photograph courtesy Zoetrope Studios. Dialogue
from the original screenplay, *Apocalypse Now,* by
John Milius and Francis Coppola. Copyright © 1979
by Omni Zoetrope. All rights reserved.

*Probably the most famous surfing artist of all time is Rick Griffin, a Southern Californian who gained notoriety during the early 1960s for his surfing cartoon character named Murphy. Griffin also is celebrated in popular culture circles as the creator of many of surfing's and rock and roll's most important early poster art. At right are pictures he created for two genre surf movies—*Five Summer Stories *(1979) and* Blazing Boards *(1983).*

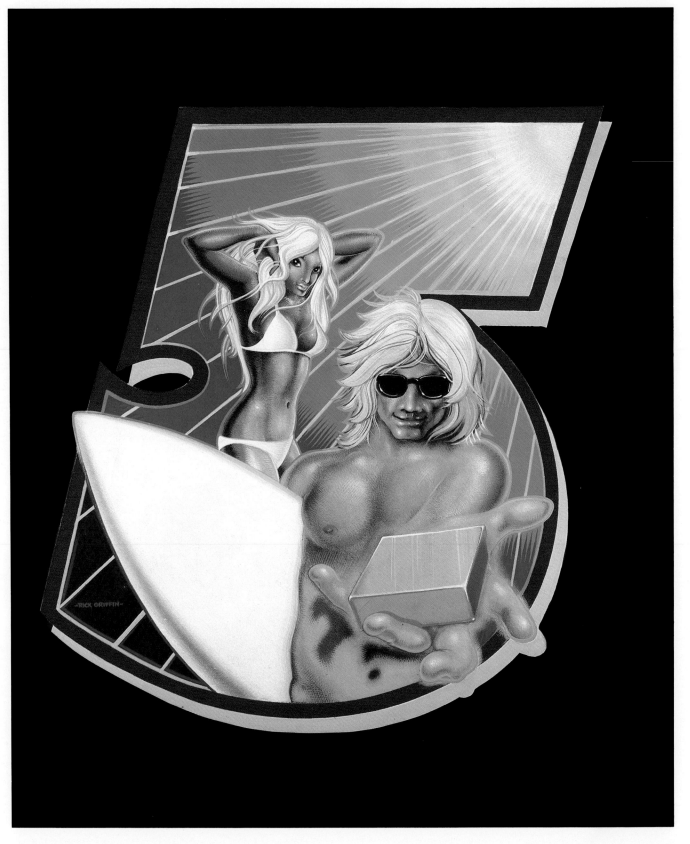

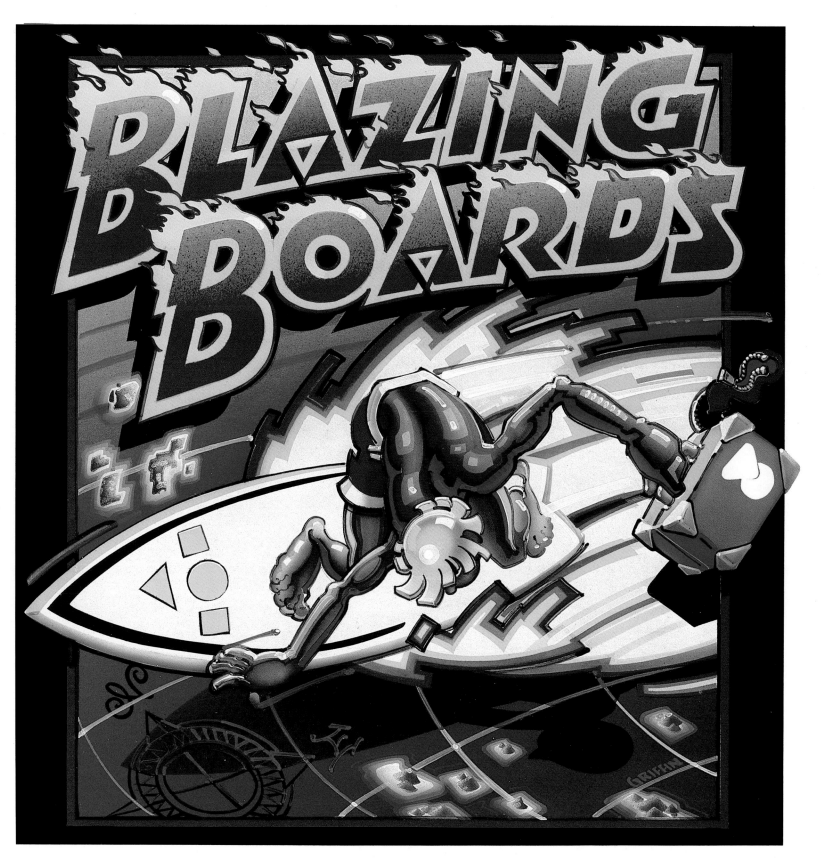

The ink and color wash pictures reproduced on these two pages were rendered by the celebrated British artist Ralph Steadman.

Steadman completed these works following a 1981 visit to Hawaii with the American "Gonzo" journalist, Dr. Hunter S. Thompson.

SURF CHIC

SURF MUSIC, beach blanket movies and related popular culture spinoffs all had varying degrees of influence on the non-surfing public-at-large. But ironically — and in a strange twist of cinematic fate — the most powerful pro-surfing medium of the Surfing Sixties was a 91-minute long, privately-produced surf movie that quietly challenged, and beat, Hollywood at its commercial and glamorous game.

We're recalling, of course, *The Endless Summer,* a charming, homemade surf flick that reached out to social worlds beyond surfing and generated a positive image and publicity windfall for the sport that is still remembered and felt twenty years later. That documentary — produced by a then 28-year-old Dana Point filmmaker named Bruce Brown — was arguably the most important and influential statement made about surfing in this century.

When *The Endless Summer* was first screened during the summer of 1964, surfing's public image was anything but healthy. The national press, which in those fragile times was ultra-conservative and squeamish about anything new and "hip," regularly painted a mental mural of surfing and surfers that dwelled on buzz words such as "beach bum," "anti-social" and "drug-induced." Even influential *Time* magazine began a January, 1964 news feature titled "Shooting the Tube" by describing the surfing phenomenon in the following semantically compromising way:

> Riding a board through the surf is a little like going on hashish. The addicts — and there are 18,000 of them in the U.S. — have their own fashions in everything from haircuts (long, but not too long) to swimsuits (cotton, a size too small). They speak a lingo of words like "hook" (the lip of a breaking wave) and "tube" (the cavern under the hook) and "wipe out" (a spill into the boiling froth). They listen to apostles, who preach: "When the surf is good, you've got to go and get it. Work is secondary. Once you're about 30, then it's time to take a solid job."

That sort of negative word-play in an international news magazine was bad enough, but an even more despicable image bummer surfaced during 1964 when the media played up a story about a pathetic cat burglar known as Jack "Murph the Surf" Murphy. Murphy had nothing to do with surfing or surfers, but his nickname made bold and memorable headlines that year after he and others were arrested and convicted for stealing a 563.35 karat "Star of India" sapphire and 21 other precious gems from New York's Museum of Natural History. The real surfing Murphy was an innocuous little cartoon gremmie created for *Surfer* magazine by California surfer-artist Rick Griffin, but for years later, whenever surfing was mentioned in non-surfing circles, people invariably smiled and recalled the sad spectacle that was "Murph the Surf," jewelry thief.

Even Tom Wolfe, that dapper "new journalist" who earns his living by flitting like a correspondent bee from groovy this to culturally aberrant that, contributed to surfing's less than wholesome, early Sixties image. Wolfe did this by composing a well-read story, *The Pump House Gang,* about La Jolla, California's hard-partying and indiscreet Mac Meda Destruction Company.

"I met a group of surfers, the Pump House Gang," Wolfe wrote in a dispatch for the *New York World Journal.* "They attended the Watts Riots as if it were the Rose Bowl game in Pasadena. They came to watch 'the drunk niggers' and were reprimanded by the same for their rowdiness."

After recounting surfing expressions and maneuvers that are idiomatically incorrect and physi-

"Young Man with Surfboard," oil on canvas, ©Wade Reynolds, 1971, reproduced courtesy of the Louis Newman Galleries, Beverly Hills, California.

Copyright © 1982 by the Marvel Comics Group. All rights reserved.

cally impossible ("Miraculously, he beat the suction. He cut back and did a spinner, which [he] followed with a reverse kick-up."), New Yorker Wolfe predicted the eventual demise of *surf chic*. He boldly prophesied that California's coastline would one day "be littered with the bodies of aged and abandoned Surferkinder, like so many beached whales." The "mysterioso mystique" of the Sixties, Wolfe said, would stagnate on West Coast beaches.

Most surfers of those times were simply out in the water "getting wet" and having a good time, but such were the condescending, negative image recalls they and the sport had to live with. However, and in spite of such untoward publicity, the sport once again survived, thanks in large part to the success of Brown's *The Endless Summer*.

Brown's delightful film — about two California surfers (Mike Hynson and Robert August) who travel about the world in search of an endless summer and *the perfect wave* — succeeded beyond his wildest (and wettest) dreams.

Filmmaker Brown had been making surf movies for nearly a decade (his first effort, 1958's *Slippery When Wet*, featuring a sophisticated soundtrack by jazz altoist Bud Shank, is a surf classic), but most of his early wave productions were of an in-house, surfy genre — that is, they catered primarily to surfers and a few curious outsiders. Many surf film purists prefer the "underground" and "pirate" nature of such movies, but few of these films ever "made it" in the outside world. Rather, they were — and still are — usually seen only by hooting, wave-crazed surfers who crowd into obscure beach town theatres and high school auditoriums to witness an endless procession of wave clips, usually soundtracked by taped rock and roll music and occasional, understated surfspeak. Indeed, it is very possible for a person to witness an entire such movie and never know what the narrator has said. Another hallmark of surf films is the notable absence of a discernible story line or theme.

Brown's more conservative and ambitious goal was to produce a surf movie that would turn everybody — non-surfers as well as surfers — on to his favorite sport. "I've always felt," he told *Los Angeles Times* writer Patrick McNulty in 1967, "that an endless summer would be the ultimate for a surfer. It's really simple to cross the equator during our winter and find summer in the Southern Hemisphere. I thought how lovely just to travel slowly around the world following summer to places like Senegal, Ghana, Nigeria, South Africa, Australia, New Zealand, Tahiti and Hawaii — and finally back to California."

Instead of just thinking such romantic and adventurous thoughts, Brown, Hynson and August did just that, and when *The Endless Summer* documentary debuted at the Santa Monica Civic Auditorium during the summer of 1964, it played to sell-out crowds for seven straight nights. "It was unbelievable — we even outdrew the Beatles," Brown recalled later.

Brown and the surfing world saw his adventure movie as "a hot property" that could draw crowds outside of surfing, but when Brown and a business associate, R. Paul Allen, courted Hollywood and New York producers and distributors, they were waved off. One New York film distributor told Allen that the movie was "non commercial." "Nice try, kid," he said, "but it won't sell 10 miles from the water."

To prove that *The Endless Summer* would sell, Brown and Allen mounted a very tough screen test. They opened the movie in Wichita, Kansas, a city about as far away from surfing as any in the United States. The movie premiered there during bad winter weather — it was snowing outside and the temperature was 2 degrees above

In surfing, nothing is more chic than a good tube ride. The gentleman ensconced in the tasty little Newport Beach tunnel at right is Bill Sharp. Responsible for this brilliant image (and the look in Sharp's eyes) was photographer Mike Moir.

zero — but despite such meteorological obstacles, it was a smash hit. As journalist McNulty reported, "For a two-week period, the film outgrossed the theater's two previous heavyweight attractions, *The Great Race* and *My Fair Lady*."

Armed with the confidence such an improbable success might inspire, Brown and Allen repaired back to New York, where they blew *The Endless Summer* film print up to 35 mm, rented the Kips Bay Theater in Lower Manhattan, and premiered their international surf movie to rave New York reviews. Even *Time* magazine gushed positively, calling *The Endless Summer* "an ode to sun, sea and sand."

The rest of this story is a fine chapter in surfing folklore. Brown's movie surfed on to great success in theaters throughout the U.S., Canada and around the world. Film critics began calling him things like the "Bergman of the boards," the "Fellini of the foam" and other such sobriquets. Brown's production budget for *The Endless Summer* was a reported $50,000, peanuts by Hollywood standards, but by May of 1967, *Variety*, the popular show business daily, was predicting that the movie would gross at least $6,000,000. That sum later grew to $8,000,000, and Brown became surfing's first movie mogul.

Brown's success was and still is laudable, but more important than his artistic and commercial achievements is what his movie did for surfing. From Duluth to Paris, *the surfer* was no longer perceived as an archetypal, anarchic beach bum or societal laze about, but rather, he became a symbol of a healthy and glamorous lifestyle that during the later Sixties, Seventies and now Eighties would greatly influence the look and tone of fashion, language and leisure time activities throughout the wet — and dry — world.

Meanwhile, as the Sixties decade matured, other important changes began occurring *within* surfing. Emerging from shaping rooms, beachside think tanks and fashion galleries were new surfing styles and equipment trends that would once again revolutionize the sport's sense of direction. Much of this new thought had to do with commercial appeal, that is, the business of selling surfboards, but it also had to do with surfing's ongoing preoccupation with aero- and hydrodynamics and man's relationship to moving bodies of wind, sea and fiberglass.

Surprisingly, or as some described it, *shockingly*, the most innovative of these experimental surfing concepts began to take crude shape in Australia, that mythical Land of Oz that sprawls lonely and by itself thousands of mind miles away from surfing's traditional shrines and legends. "Australia?" surfers asked back then, wondering what kangaroos and fermented yeast paste had to do with hanging ten and getting tubed.

Yes, mate, Australia. Surfing's Northern Hemisphere historians hate to admit it, but beginning in the mid-1960s and continuing until sometime early in 1982, America — and all tasty surf zones, north, south, east and west of Down Under — were rudely assaulted and all but subdued by an "Aussie Invasion" of bronzed, talented and inordinately aggressive wavecrackers.

It's hard to pinpoint just when the earnest Aussies began preparing for this invasion, but as early as 1958, America's original surf moviemaker, Bud Browne, visited that country and filmed the first stirrings of a "modern" surf culture there. His 1958 movie, *Surf Down Under*, was the first truly international surf film ever made.

While in Aussie-land, Browne screened several of his best Fifties surf movies, and for the first time, Australians sat up in loge seats and studied the hotdogging moves and scary, spewing walls of water that made Malibu, Makaha and other such California-Hawaii surf spots famous. Probably

Posing, left, with his "Christmas Quiver" is North Shore habitue Jeff Crawford. Like many serious surfers, Crawford has a board made for every possible wave condition he might want to experience.

within hours of seeing such things, young, tow-headed grommets were out in the water on their "Malibus," trying, trying, to climb and drop like the Yanks from San Onofre and Sunset.

During the next few years, these travel-prone Australians were on surfari to Hawaii and California. And by 1962, one of the more talented of their lot, Bernard "Midget" Farrelly, competed in — and won! — the annual Makaha International Surfing Championships meet hosted by the Waikiki Surf Club. Two years later, at a first big World Contest, held in 1964 at Manly Beach, Sydney, home-towner Farrelly again placed first, this time ahead of Hawaii-based Joey Cabell and Californian Mike Doyle. Farrelly won fair and square, but Californians and Hawaiians who attended and competed in the World Contest attributed his win to "a home court advantage."

"Fair dinkum?" Farrelly's critics asked, scratching their sun-bleached hair, but two years later, at a third World Contest, this one held in the San Diego area, those same Yankee skeptics turned silent.

The usually arrogant Americans were rendered speechless because that 1966 world meet was not just won, but brutally dominated, by yet another Australian. This time Robert "Nat" Young, the so-called "Animal" from New South Wales, showed up at San Diego bearing a "short," chopped down surfboard, and proceeded to literally blow away his American competitors in their back yard. Big, sinewy Nat, riding a 9'4", 22" wide and very thin (for those times) board he called "Magic Sam," powered and graced his way past the world's best surfers in a way nobody could believe.

Drew Kampion, an assistant editor of *Surfing* magazine, recalled in a recent, latter-day commentary on that World Contest that Young's performance at San Diego marked the dawning of "an era of Australian dominance" of competitive surfing and the first "crumbling" of surfing's "California mystique." Young's new, short board power-surfing, Kampion said, signaled a "commercial and ideological threat [that] was so huge that no one dared mention it. In fact, the Aussies themselves had to come out and beat their own chests and boast their own eminence; otherwise the surfing world seemed bound and determined to ignore them and dismiss [the] San Diego [contest] as a fluke."

Surfing thus began a long and complicated drop into its current "short board era," and in the years since, surfers — even non-Australian surfers — have been doing things on waves that were undreamed of during the times of *Gidget*, Longboard Legends and toes on the nose. The average length of a surfboard shrank from about 10 feet in 1964 to about 6 feet by 1970, and along with this accelerated shrinkage emerged styles of aggressive attack, air-whipping, high performance surfing that bear little resemblance to anything that preceded them. Or as *Surfing*'s Kampion so eloquently expresses it: "After years of gradual evolution in materials and design and maneuvers, suddenly everything was changed; suddenly the surfboard was a mind-vehicle that you could project where you wanted it; it was like being set free."

Set free? When it came to Australians, it was more like being unleashed. While their laid-back American counterparts were getting stoned, humping in Vietnam and "soul surfing" in non-ego "expression sessions," the go for bloke, meat-eating Aussies went for "organized" surfing's jugular vein. For more than a decade, they zig-zagged and blasted their way to surfing prominence. "Bustin' down the door," they called their contest-sweeping antics, and a transcontinental surfing war was on. With senior officers Farrelly and Young paving the way, other, younger recruits

The arresting mood photo at left is a portrait by Art Brewer of the late Adolph Bunker Spreckles III. Spreckles was the archetypal California surfer — tanned, blonde and in lean and ready surfing condition.

153

In a seemingly nonplussed surf ski moment, Herbie Fletcher leaps high over more conventional surfers waiting for waves at Southern California's Lower Trestles surf spot. This particular surf machine is powered by a 500 cc bored out engine of Fletcher's design.

such as Cheyne Horan ("The Blonde Bombshell from Bondi"), Wayne "Rabbit" Bartholomew and Mark "SuperSurfer" Richards mounted a formidable set piece and pincer attack on Up There.

Richards was particularly impressive. Riding a provocative twin fin short board embellished with a big "MR" deck decal that evoked Superman's "S" logo, he exhibited radical surfing maneuvers that during the late Seventies and early Eighties earned him an unprecedented four world titles in a row. The only "foreign" waverider who even came close to MR during his 1979–1982 Golden Era was a streaking new performer from South Africa named Shaun Thomson.

Front doors, back doors, trap doors — all were methodically punched in by the disciplined Aussie blitzkrieg. Until just recently, that is. In late 1982 and early 1983, those wide open surfing doors began turning into a frozen revolving door as a vengeful and disparate squad of cool young Californians, Hawaiians and South Africans began slashing back. As 1983's waves began crashing, stylistic hotties like California's Tommy Curren, Hawaii's Hans Hedemann, Michael Ho and Dane Kealoha, and South Africa's Thomson and Martin Potter began giving the Aussies the proverbial boot. Nobody's sure how long this counterattack will sustain itself, but as of this book's printing Australia's long held surfing cup was beginning to run dry.

Yes, the tide runs in, the tide runs out. But what is one to make of this "Aussie Invasion," revolutionary short boards, the long-awaited "Non-Aussie Backlash" and surfing's new "freedom to fly"? What do such esoteric bits of surfiana mean? Does anybody really care about friendly shootouts, ala *High Noon,* in which the weapons of choice are V-bottoms, twin fins, tri fins and, more recently, swallow-winged thrusters with clusters? Is professionalism really dead?

Surfing's newest "oldtimers" — meaning anybody over the age of 35 — will tell you that all the above are part of a surfing media hype designed to sell ever-changing surfboards and give surfing magazines something to write about. That may be partially true, but remember also that young "slash and burn" artists, not unlike their noseriding elders, become very serious, almost psychoanalytical, when discussing their waveriding "art." They are as obsessed with "going for air" and "cranking 360s" as their fathers were with "hanging five" and "stalling through sections." The equipment and jargon may change, but the beat, the rhythm, goes on . . .

Indeed, from "Pray For Surf" in the Sixties to "In God We Thrust" in the Eighties, surfing's confident young thoroughbreds have maintained a constant, agitated state of change. The modern surfer, like other earthly transcendents, is not content to stand statue-like, as author London expressed it, with "the salt smoke rising to his knees." Instead, he wants to get "rad"; his nihilistic goal is to push his joyous, identification-with-nature life to a new, adrenalized, locked-in-the-green-room extreme.

Certain of these rubber-bodied waveriders think nothing of banking off the bottom of a wave like an erratic rocket and carving a full 360-degree track across a glassy, fast-breaking face. And other, more adventurous souls prefer soaring off a wave's lip and into a seemingly impossible display of "aerial" aquatics. Not that barrel-rolling tube rides are no longer *de rigueur,* but why keep doing the same thing — if you know you can do it.

As this nervy dance of life raced on before mini-rainbowed spindrifts, even more complicated, tribal-like rituals evolved and endured on shore. As the outside world drove by, surfing's roaming, phallus-riding subculture interrelated, grew and established itself as a community.

Close your eyes and imagine a tribe of surfers in their quonset hut longhouses on Oahu's North Shore. It's the end of a long, hard day of surfriding, and these exhausted, sunburnt aboriginals have paused to eat, rest and prepare for another day's assault on nature. In front rooms adorned with the icons, totems and relics of their sect are the grunting, satisfied men. As alcoholic beverages and hash pipes are passed from male to male, each mutters wave-inspired idioms unintelligible to outside observers. Meanwhile, in other living areas, the "surfer girls," the women, quietly shuffle about, nursing babies and preparing the evening's communal feast.

This *National Geographic* scenario is not entirely accurate, but makes for an amusing analogy. Though the surfing lifestyle is not *primitive* per se, it is distinctly subcultural and — from an anthropological perspective — not too unlike other cultish societies that exhibit unique modes of dress, language and bodily adornment. As do other homogeneous and non-secular societies, this wave-ridden culture assigns great value to physical prowess, craftsmanship and, as alluded above, male chauvinism.

Take a look at the much thumbed through surfing literature that lies sprawled about in a surfer's living compound. In these sacred periodicals one finds scores of scantily clad "surfer girls" who do not — as a rule — have names. Rather, these aggregate shes are "bikini winners," "attractive spectators" or "local fauns." Ahh-roooh! the men shout, and a Beach Boys song moans, "Do you love me, do you surfer girl."

Conversely, a wave is not *just* a wave, but "pure unsweetened island juice" in the "sparkle room" of a "moving castle" pounded by "rolling thunder." And ahh-rooh again, true believers, because one does not simply surf; one "slamma jams," "shreds," "carves," "sizzles" and "slashes."

Additionally, a wave is not measured in units of feet, but "in increments of fear." Those big "bluebirds," as Hawaii oldtimers called 'em, don't look like much from shore, but paddle out there, brah, and you too will be baptized, terrified and made to believe. Or mo bettah, go easy. Just watch. Stand on the cliffs at Waimea Bay, like a spectator at Rome's Colosseum, and hoot out loud as twenty to thirty-foot north swells lift like glossy black holes on the blue-grey horizon. Watch — while City and County fire engines with ominous revolving red and yellow lights stand by and wait for a casualty call; while the ground shudders underfoot; and while surfing's madmen paddle into an awesome lineup, wheel around, and freefall into Adrenalin City.

Heady stuff this — but why do it? Why risk being pile driven into an undersea garden of jagged coral heads? Why freeze your ass in offshore waters during a New England winter? Why?

Some surfing metaphysicians attribute the sport's attraction to an intimidating "outlaw charm" that can't be matched by more restrictive and "organized" forms of recreation. On God's wave, they say, you are truly free and with Him.

Alvin Toffler, the pop futurist, wrote in his best-selling book, *Future Shock*, that the surfing life — and its variously manifested eccentricities, nomadic lifestyle and fashionable trappings — represents a wave of the future. The sport, he says, gives its men, women and hangers-on a much-needed *sense of identity* and a tacit *freedom to be different.*

"The number of acceptable games, sports and entertainments is climbing rapidly," he said, "and the growth of a distinct subcult built around surfing, for example, demonstrates that at least for some, a leisure time commitment can serve as the basis for an entire lifestyle. The surfing subcult is a signpost pointing towards the future."

In recent months, surf photographers have begun taking to the water with sophisticated flash synch camera systems. This particular tube ride was flash photographed by California camera man Chuck Schmid. On target at Venice Beach is surfer Alan Sarlo.

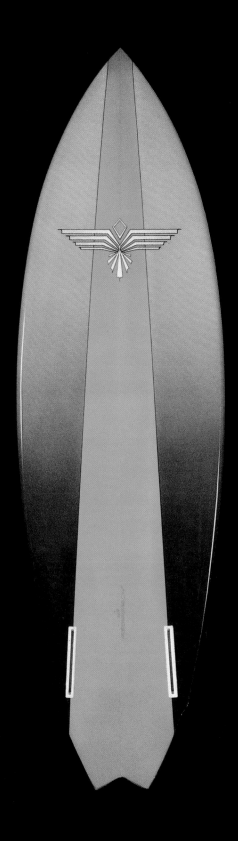

Surfboard shapers and glassers have long been recognized in wave-riding circles as design artists. To wit, an Eighties equipment sampler: From left, a double wing pin twin fin by Nectar Surfboards (airbrushed by Henry Lund); a traditional pintail by Aqua Surfboards (shaper, Rod Sorenson); a swallow winger twin fin by Canyon Surfboards (shaper-airbrusher, Rus Preisendorfer); and a pintail Ranch Special by Nectar Surfboards (shaped and designed by Rick Tumilty).

PROFESSIONALS CASH IN

As long ago as the Middle Ages, surf contests were held in Hawaii, and when a champion emerged triumphant from the day's waves, he or she was lavished with valuable properties, floral wreaths (*leis*) and other such prizes. Meanwhile, on the sidelines, spectators cheered and indulged themselves in high stakes gambling by betting valuable personal effects on a favored surfer.

Hawaiian folks no longer entertain odds on talented waveriders, but during the past two decades of surfing's development, more refined attempts have been made worldwide to "professionalize" the sport.

Surfing historians recall that nominal money prizes were awarded as early as 1965, notably at a Tom Morey invitational "noseriding" contest held that year at Ventura, California, but it wasn't until 1969 that cash was awarded at a properly staged professional surf meet. This was at a contest held annually in honor of the late Duke Paoa Kahanamoku. In the winter of '69, on the occasion of the Fifth Annual Duke Kahanamoku Invitational Surfing Championships (renamed that year the Duke Kahanamoku Hawaiian Surfing Classic), meet producer Kimo Wilder McVay, in cooperation with CBS television producer Larry Lindbergh, posted a first place prize of $1,000. Surfing's first big pro winner was a Californian, Mike Doyle, and a picture of him receiving his cash prize in a traditional Hawaiian calabash bowl stands as an important visual landmark in the history of modern professional surfing.

The response of surfers — and the public — to the idea of professional surfing meets added a more hard core, competitive edge to the drama of a surfing contest, so in the next few years this riding-for-cash concept became more and more popular and lucrative.

In 1970, Hawaiian surfer-businessman Fred Hemmings contributed and raised some $6,000 for a first Smirnoff Pro-Am meet sponsored by the Heublein Corporation and held at Hawaii's Makaha Beach. Surfers arrived from all parts of the world for this meet, and a $3,000 first prize was carried away by Nat Young, an aggressive, power-surfer from Australia.

Following those promising pro starts, yet a third moneyed meet, the Pipeline Masters, was held in 1971 at Hawaii's spectacular Banzai Pipeline. Six top tuberiders were invited to compete, and this time Jeff Hakman, a dimunitive but canny Hawaiian waverider, took the prize money and ran. The organizer was again Hemmings, and his first two productions were so well-received that pro surfing began to attract the attention of yet other television networks (this time ABC and NBC).

Before those first three pro meets, contest surfing was more a matter of prestige and ego satisfaction than a quest for monetary reward. If anything, competitive surfing before that time had a wholesome, nearly Olympian air about it. The only commercial rewards were surfboards, occasional modeling fees and related equipment benefits given to surfers by surfboard and ocean wear manufacturers. If a contest winner was lucky, and properly promoted, he or she might make a few extra dollars by attaching his or her name to a line of surfboards or swimwear.

Meanwhile, in faraway Australia, yet other surfers, sponsors and promoters got their surfing acts together and began producing a series of surfing contests that featured money as an incentive. A prime and initial example was the Bell's Beach (Victoria) Classic that since 1962 had been conducted as a purely amateur affair. In 1973, an Australian sportswear company, Rip Curl, offered cash benefits to the winners of that year's Bell's Classic. Then, in 1974, an even bigger and more organized affair was financed by Australian radio station Radio 2SM and the Coca-Cola bottling

On preceding pages, an attentive North Shore (Hawaii) gallery catches island rays and Banzai Pipeline action during a recent Pipeline Masters competition; left, California surf star Tommy Curren finds himself covered by a more elegant type of whitewater following a recent professional contest victory.

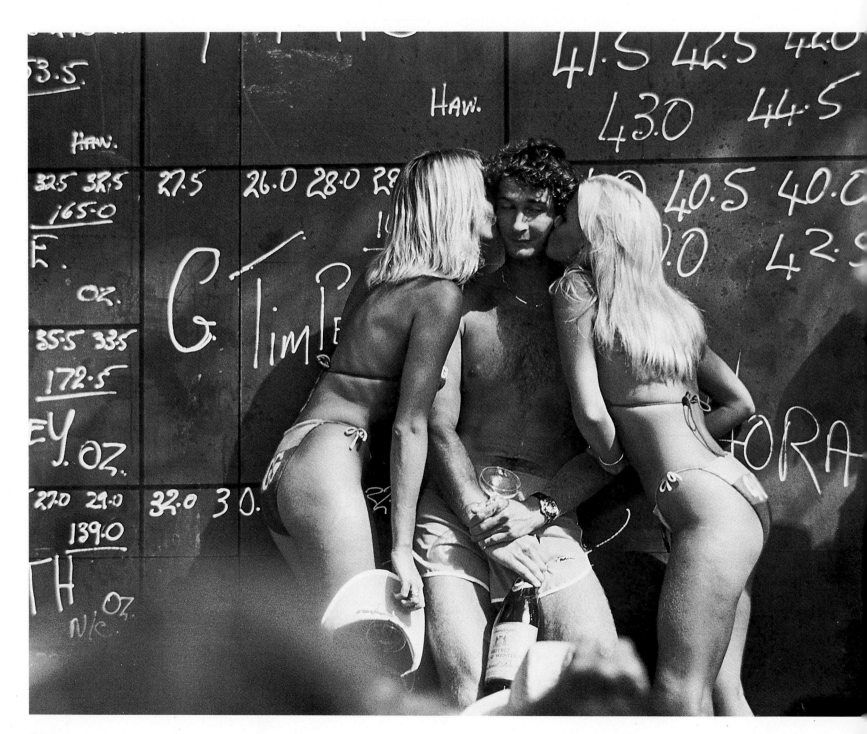

company of Sydney. Those two sponsors put up $7,000 in contest money for a roving meet held at Warriewood, Narrabeen and Manly Beach's Fairy Bower. A $3,000 first place purse was won by Australian Michael Peterson, and Down Under's blokes were off and pro $urfing.

That 2SM/Coca-Cola Bottlers Surfabout grew even bigger the next year, 1975, when Australian Wayne Lynch earned $3,500 for his contest surfing. As a sidelight, the meet inspired the formation of an Australian Professional Surfing Association to promote the efforts of professional Australian surfers at home and abroad.

The Surfabout grew cash-wise with every passing year, and by 1980 it featured some $42,000 and a motorcar as prizes, making it the richest single pro meet in surfing to date. The 1980 winner, Buzzy Kerbox, of Kailua, Hawaii, surfed about in fine island form and took some $12,000 and a new car back to the islands as contest booty.

Meanwhile, back in 1975, a group of Hawaii-based surfing entrepreneurs — Hemmings, Randy Rarick and Jack Shipley — formed a new, professionally-oriented, non-profit association they called the International Professional Surfers (IPS). This organization superseded a former International Surfing Federation (ISF) that had for years monitored the staging, judging and ethics of amateur world championship surfing meets that had been held at Peru (1965), San Diego (1966), California and Puerto Rico (1968), Australia (1970) and a second time at California (1972). The purpose of the IPS was to establish an international professional rating system and a series of by-laws and contest rules that would unify the various pro meets then being held at such diverse places as Hawaii, California, Australia, South Africa and Peru. What was being set up, in effect, was a World Circuit concept similar to that of PGA golfers or Grand Prix race drivers.

The IPS was a good idea, but fell victim to surf politics and other such bottom line intrigues. It tried hard to "organize" world surfing, but by the end of 1982 was superseded by yet another "professional" group, this one financed by an American sportswear manufacturer, the Ocean Pacific (OP) company. The new body was called the Association of Surfing Professionals (ASP), and its California-based organizers, Australian surfers Ian Cairns and Peter Townend, were working hard to keep it afloat and viable as this book was being printed.

The future of professional surfing is uncertain and debatable, but by the winter of 1983–1984, its potential cash rewards were growing steadily. As of early 1984, some $500,000 in cash prizes were available to surfers on the annual pro circuit tour of Australia, California, New Jersey, Japan, South Africa, Brazil, France, England, Indonesia (Bali) and other places.

That's not much by world sporting standards, but enough to keep surfing's elite in shape and aggressive. Consider the earnings of Californian Tommy Curren at a Straight Talk Tyres Open (sponsored by a chain of Australian *tyre* stores) held at Cronulla Beach near Sydney in April, 1983. For his Aussie surfing efforts, Curren paddled away with $18,000 in cash and a $12,000 Datsun station wagon. In Hawaii later that year, yet another hot pro, the Hawaiian Michael Ho, participated in three prestigious "Triple Crown" meets held in Hawaii's challenging North Shore winter surf and earned $16,100 by placing first in a Sunkist World Cup meet, second place in the Offshore Pipeline Masters and second place in the important Duke Classic.

As professional surfing pioneer Fred Hemmings summed it up, "That's not bad for two weeks of surfing."

"Two girls for every boy," promised a Sixties surf song refrain, and here we see what the lyrics meant as Australian surfing champion Mark Richards receives a proper Surf City congratulations. Shy Mark is used to such accolades, having won world surfing titles in 1979, 1980, 1981 and again in 1982.

KA NALU

Eia ke kū mai nei ka nalu nui
He 'onaulu loa
Ho'ohua Kūhela i ke awakea
A pae ku'u papa i ka 'ako'ako
Lele lā ka pola i ke ehu o ke kai
'O ka 'iwa kani le'a ko'u like
Kikaha ana lā i luna loa
Ho'okahi nō na'e māhiehie
Aia i ka po'ina 'ale
Me he mahiole ali'i lā
E kau ana i ka lae

Here now a big wave rises
An 'onaulu loa, a wave of great length and endurance
It swells, sweeping unbroken in the noon-day sun
My board mounts the crest
My loincloth flys in the spray of the sea
I am like the 'iwa bird crying wildly
As it soars so high above
But the finest delight
Is there in the wave's cresting
Like a royal feathered helmet
Upon my brow

— composed in Hawaiian and translated into English
by Larry Lindsey Kimura, October 12, 1983.

Steve Wilkings' Waimea Bay shorebreak study (preceding pages) vividly demonstrates why ancient and contemporary Hawaiian scholars have devoted so much fine poetry to the breaking wave. Other crashing, sparkling and tubing points of reference include Stewart Ferriman, right, as he hits a crystalline backwash lip at Makaha Beach; a North Shore tube occupied by a more-than-casual Brian Buckley (170–171); a momentary panic in pintail park (172–173); state-of-the-art wipeouts (174–175); and fine studies of Hawaiian aquatics at the Banzai Pipeline (176) and at Makaha Beach (177).

Between sets at California's Redondo breakwater, the winter of '83.

And meanwhile, on Hawaii's playful North Shore, it's standing room only.

Where there's surf, you'll find surfers, no matter how urbane the situation. Right, a pack of jetty rats scramble for space at Newport Beach.

181

During the past decade, wandering surfers have concentrated much of their peripatetic, wave-seeking energy on the Indonesian island of Bali. In this fanciful painting, titled "Kuta Beach," contemporary wave and jet sets commingle with traditional Balinese villagers and fisher folk. The artist, I Gusti Putu Sana of the highland village of Pengosekan, completed this Chinese ink study during the summer of 1972. Like a thoughtful photojournalist, Gusti zeroed in on singular subjects which in his painting communicate a busy but charming blend of spirituality, beauty and whimsy. Documentary detail verily crawls, flies, jets, leaps, hangs and yawns from every corner, mountain, temple, pond and tree in his work. A *bemo* beeps, *bir* Bintangs clink, *kreteks* crackle and pop, cameras click, and exotically saronged surfers pose and preen atop blossoming wave crests. In the right foreground, Gusti — who had never before seen this sea dance called surfing — sits on Kuta's sand and completes preliminary sketches.

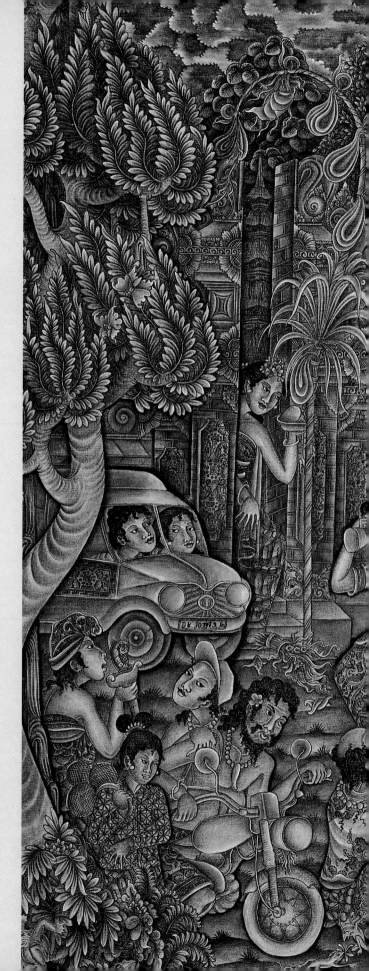

WAVES FROM ABROAD

W HEN I ROLLED into the broad and strangely empty streets of Cadiz it was late afternoon, and after finding a cheap place to stay (less than seventy five cents per day, including meals) it was too dark to check out the local beaches, so I did the next best thing. I found the nearest sidewalk bar advertising San Miguel beer. The surfboard atop my car roused the usually sleepy waiter into conversation, and after several beers together — as I was his only customer — his questions finally led to a full explanation of surfing . . ."
— *Bill Cleary*, in "Olé — Las Olas!"
from the September, 1963 issue of Surf Guide *magazine*

Southern Spain's barkeeps are probably still as astonished and intrigued by visiting surfers as they were in the summer of '63, but these days, well, so are local folks in places like Morocco, the Azores, Uruguay and southern Kyushu. *Senor* Cleary, one of surfing's earliest and finest travel writers, may indeed have been the first *Norté Americano* to drop into Atlantic waves west of Cadiz, but he certainly wasn't the last. Since those early Sixties days when most California, Hawaii and Australia "locals" went on vicarious surfaris only in the pages of *Surf Guide* and *Surfer*, thousands of the sport's most adventurous practitioners have traveled, surfed and, in the process, remapped and renamed many of the world's most remote and never-before-surfed coastlines.

Not unlike religious pilgrims who roam from one holy place to another seeking truth and salvation, the surfer — that is, the surfer who is committed to his sport — has also become a roaming, romantic seeker of truth, beauty and waves. He has been known to circumnavigate the globe in an obsessive quest for his own special *nirvana* — perfect (and uncrowded) surf spots.

Non-surfing laymen might consider this a rather exorbitant and frivolous way to spend one's time, energy and money, but surfers laugh quietly at such non-believers and paddle boldly into uncertain seas. Indeed, if a Buddhist mendicant's idea of bliss is to be alone, chanting sutras in a cold Himalayan niche, the surfer's vision of pure stoke is also to be alone, but crouching in a hot tubing reef break somewhere east of Java.

From southern France's Chambre d'Amour to Bali's Uluwatu, you'll find gypsy-like surf rats hanging out, soaking up local culture and having the climbing and dropping times of their lives.

Such serendipitous surfaris may begin simply, say as an extended dawn patrol in waters near a surfer's home town. But eventually, as the siren call of new surfing thrills draws one farther and farther from more familiar reefs, points and beachbreaks, the surfer packs his board and a few belongings and moves on. The lure of different kinds of waves, and new surfing challenges, takes him away from "home" in ever broadening circles of his special play.

Back in the Sixties, surfers were first inspired to visit exotic playgrounds by surf movies and dispatches such as the one by Cleary. Initially, their numbers were small; but wherever they went, these first surfing internationalists charmed the locals with their aquatic wizardry and, oftentimes, even paused to teach some of the spectators how to surf. Remember that fun-filled scene in *The Endless Summer* in which Californians Mike Hynson and Robert August gave surfing lessons to a throng of laughing Ghanian kids? It was one of the greatest social icebreakers ever captured on film.

Even so-called civilized societies respond with mirth and amazement. In a July, 1963 *Surf Guide* piece titled "If You Blokes Wanta Ride Some Real Bloody Crunchers, Get Yer Arse to Cornwall," peripatetic Cleary recounts how he and a group of Aussie waveriders verily terrified a crowd of se-

A small school of friendly dolphins protects a stylized surfer from an evil sea creature in this dance-like study of surfing by I. Made Budi of Batuan, Bali.

Surfer-skier Gerard D' Auezac glides left at Hossegor, just north of Biarritz on France's Atlantic Coast.

date British surfbathers by riding in that ancient resort's "tubing beauties."

After paying six bob (then about 85 cents) to enter Cornwall's formal bathing area, he and his Aussie friends (Ian Tilley, John Campbell, Bob Head and Warren Mitchell) casually paddled out through Cornwall's more conservative surfbathers and proceeded to put the day's throngs "in turmoil." Or as Cleary reported:

> English surfing consists of riding the inside whitewater on their plastic breadboards, and these crazy Australians paddling out into the churning maelstrom disturbed the equilibrium of the usually reserved British to the point of panic. They immediately summoned lifeguards, fire trucks, ambulance, and even the sea watch helicopter that patrols the Cornwall Coast. The frenzied populace was gathered en masse on the beach, fearing for the lives of the boys . . . .

The Brits' well-intended panic eventually subsided, Cleary explained, when the sea watch helicopter's captain assured fellow citizens "that the bloomin' idiots were playing out there . . . that they were laughing and having a jolly old time of it."

In many places where surfers have come, surfed and gone, the sport has been picked up and even perfected by stoked locals. One particularly good example is the island of Bali, which since the early Seventies has become one of surfing's favorite foreign destinations. On that culturally rich East Indonesian island, surfing has not only been enthusiastically embraced by local youths, but has developed to the point where the island's resort areas now include active surf shops, surf boutiques, surf clubs, and even a big annual surf contest that's part of surfing's interna-

Deux modes de transport— *below, at Uluwatu, Bali, and right, at the Club Waikiki, Peru.*

Hawaiian pro surfer Buzzy Kerbox cuts back and into a picture perfect wave inside South Africa's sail-filled Bay of Plenty.

tional professional competition circuit. This development is even more astonishing when you consider that in recent times the average Hindu Balinese would rarely ever swim in coastal waters. The sea, according to their beliefs, is a "dark" place populated by evil creatures and the disconcerted spirits of the Balinese dead.

Other geographical areas where surfing has become established and a regular part of local, beachside culture are Peru, France, South Africa and the Indian Ocean islands of Mauritius and the Seychelles. The sport has also been well-received throughout Latin America, the Caribbean, the Philippines, Portugal and in Micronesia.

Remember the war in Vietnam? Sure, but how many of you remember the Allied Surf Association of the South China Sea? This little-known surf club was made up of surfing grunts who took "R & R" from jungle firefights by riding waves at Nha Trang and Vung Tau. This Aussie-Yank association was formed, wrote a member in 1968, "to exchange surf stories and ideas, but the membership is not very stable, what with business commitments being what they've been lately."

Exotic waveriding, yes, but nowhere outside of America, Australia, New Zealand and South Africa has the sport been so cultishly adopted in recent years as it has been in that new Land of the Rising Surf, Japan. During the late Seventies and early Eighties, the trend-prone Japanese have taken to surfing like New York has taken to *sushi*. Nobody's sure just how big the surfing industry really is there, but in early 1984 you could find more surf shops in the greater Tokyo-Yokohama-Kamakura area than in all of Hawaii.

The place is not exactly ridden with waves, but the Japanese have made the most of what they've got. The Sea of Japan usually provides mere ankle-breaking ripples, but on any given Sunday these days, you'll find veritable hordes of so-

Ubiquitous traffic and a famous red torii gate frame a squad of well-equipped City Surfers found at Kamakura, Japan.

called "City Surfers" out in the water on the latest imported and custom-shaped surfing gear.

A Tokyo CBS television correspondent recalls the scene there in June of 1983 when he and a visiting CBS camera crew filmed a very successful short spot on surfing in Japan. "We found a surfer's bar, surfers' boutiques and surf shops galore, but when we went to the beach to see a crew of surfers, there were no waves. We asked a surfer what was going on, and he explained, 'In Japan, we call this fashion-surfing.'"

Despite such quaint and trendy adversity, many young Japanese have become quite adept at surfing, and in the process have spearheaded the development of a distinctly Japanese surfing subculture. Numerous surfing magazines have begun appearing on newsstands there, newer and better surf spots have been discovered, and a chic new fashion wave based on surfing has had a profound effect on the country's perception of *surfer style*. There's even a popular magazine, *Fine,* that advertises itself as a "Sea-Side Date" for rosy-cheeked "Surfer Girls."

The Western surfing media are not sure what all this internationalizing of surfing will mean for the sport in years to come, but in the case of Japan, it is certainly solid, commercial evidence that the sport is alive, thriving and hasn't lost its popular and romantic appeal.

Politically, surfing has managed to remain relatively pure and blind to the world's greater social problems — except on the rare occasion when surfers have experienced incidents of unreasonable racism or "this is my surf" territoriality.

A poignant case in point concerns the 1972 visit to South Africa by the late and much-admired Hawaiian surfer Eddie Aikau. When dark-skinned Aikau arrived in that country during the summer of '72 to compete in a big Durban 500 surfing meet, he was astonished to find that he was being dis-

California surfer Ray Chapman, right, confronts a crystal lip he found at San Quintin in Baja California. Also framed in this Aaron Chang travel photograph is a neat lineup of extinct Baja volcanoes.

criminated against and was a victim of the South African government's strict apartheid policies.

To begin with, Aikau's participation in the Durban meet was mysteriously postponed until the last possible moment amid speculation that his skin color would cause "problems." Then, though he was eventually invited to compete in the 500, upon his arrival he was inexplicably segregated from other, lighter-skinned surfers. Instead of joining other more *haole* members of Hawaii's surfing team in their headquarters hotel, he was arbitrarily put up in an inn some 12 miles away from his friends and the contest site.

"I was all on my own there. During the day, nobody asked 'Where are you going? Is somebody taking you around?' I was going against my own people. They forgot me," Aikau later told Pierre Bowman, a reporter for the *Honolulu Star-Bulletin*.

In the end, Aikau was "saved" by local friends he made while in his dark and solitary confinement, but the memory of that experience stayed with him — and haunted him — until the time he died in a freak maritime accident in March of 1978.

Yes, surfing has its untoward moments, but the dedicated, traveling surfer is still out there — wandering, looking, searching for that *perfect wave*. The world is his woodie, waves are his drug, and there's more of both than he'll ever be able to experience in a lifetime.

Paul Holmes, the British-born and well-traveled editor of *Surfer* magazine, says the traveling surfer is one of the world's most-interesting types of travelers "because he's always traveling with a definite goal or purpose."

"Unlike many travelers," says Holmes, "the surfer always knows what he wants, why he wants it, and where to find it. He's not — like some people on the so-called 'Hippie Trail' — an anxious and aimless wanderer with no particular place to go."

'WINDSURFING' TAKES OFF

Beneath the grand, sweeping trade-winds of the Pacific, across the breathy heat of the legendary *sirocco* of the Mediterranean, and here and there between the Roaring Forties and Howling Fifties, there's something "new" and surfing-related going on that bears special notice. That phenomenon is an exciting world class watersport that is popularly referred to as boardsailing (and, in a strictly commercial or idiomatic context, as "windsurfing"). After more than two decades of international regattas and high-powered financing and publicity, this third cousin to surfing and sailing has been so well-received by the planet's sports community that it was recently added as a seventh class in Olympic yachting, just in time for the 1984 Olympic Games at Los Angeles. Boardsailing's origins are a matter of conjecture, but as long ago as 1935, Tom Blake, the celebrated surfing pioneer, rigged a crude, lateen sail to a streamlined, hollow paddleboard and let her fly in Hawaiian winds. "The contraption ran well before the wind. [But] when he got to sea, he turned around and tried to sail home. He couldn't sail against the wind. So he paddled back," wrote Honolulu journalist Richard Weinberg in 1941. Blake, not one to be daunted or caught in irons, kept experimenting with the device, and eventually, with the addition of a keel and a foot-controlled rudder, he developed a "sailing surfboard" that would indeed work with and against the wind. In March of 1941, a "first official surfboard sailing race in yachting history" was held off Waikiki's Outrigger Canoe Club. It featured 10 sailboards of what Blake called the Iwa Class. Blake named his sailing surfboards Iwas after the Hawaiian name, *Iwa,* for the majestic frigate bird "which glides effortlessly across the sky with wings shaped like a 'w.'" On the occasion of that historic regatta, Blake predicted that this fledgling sport would spread to other parts of the world and lend even greater fame to surfing, sailing and watersports in general. Little did mild-mannered Blake — and others on the beach that day — realize that more than 40 years later (and following numerous equipment innovations by other, more enterprising persons) boardsailing would evolve into "the fastest-growing leisure sport in the world."

A camera mounted high in the mast —and fired by remote control —places the viewer deep into the action of wavejumping off Diamond Head, Oahu, Hawaii.

APPENDICES

EVOLUTION OF THE SURFBOARD

SURF MUSIC

A SURF FILMOGRAPHY

BIBLIOGRAPHY

INDEX

CREDITS / ACKNOWLEDGMENTS

This ethereal, underwater vision of body surfers at Makapuu, Hawaii, was captured by Honolulu photo artist Wayne Levin.

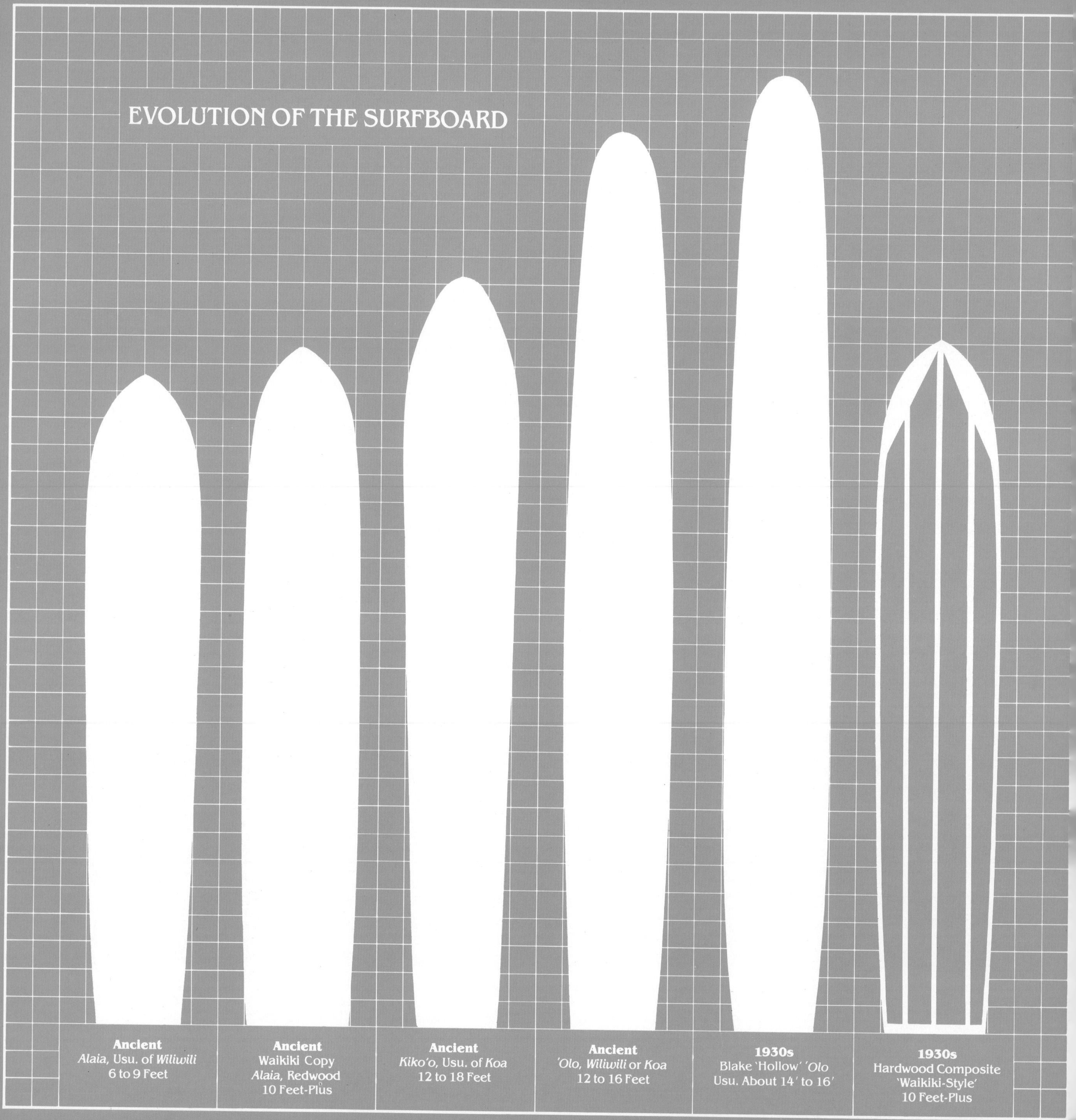

EVOLUTION OF THE SURFBOARD

Ancient
Alaia, Usu. of *Wiliwili*
6 to 9 Feet

Ancient
Waikiki Copy
Alaia, Redwood
10 Feet-Plus

Ancient
Kiko'o, Usu. of *Koa*
12 to 18 Feet

Ancient
'Olo, Wiliwili or *Koa*
12 to 16 Feet

1930s
Blake 'Hollow' *'Olo*
Usu. About 14' to 16'

1930s
Hardwood Composite
'Waikiki-Style'
10 Feet-Plus

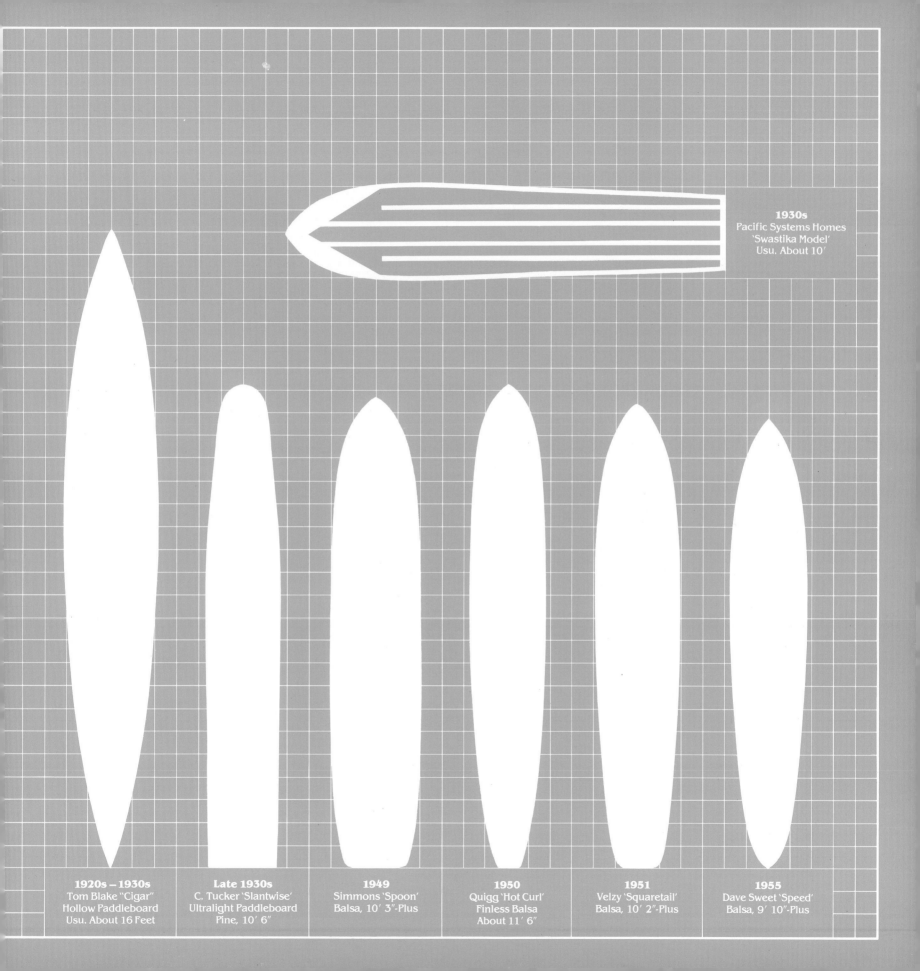

1930s
Pacific Systems Homes
'Swastika Model'
Usu. About 10′

1920s–1930s
Tom Blake "Cigar"
Hollow Paddleboard
Usu. About 16 Feet

Late 1930s
C. Tucker 'Slantwise'
Ultralight Paddleboard
Pine, 10′ 6″

1949
Simmons 'Spoon'
Balsa, 10′ 3″-Plus

1950
Quigg 'Hot Curl'
Finless Balsa
About 11′ 6″

1951
Velzy 'Squaretail'
Balsa, 10′ 2″-Plus

1955
Dave Sweet 'Speed'
Balsa, 9′ 10″-Plus

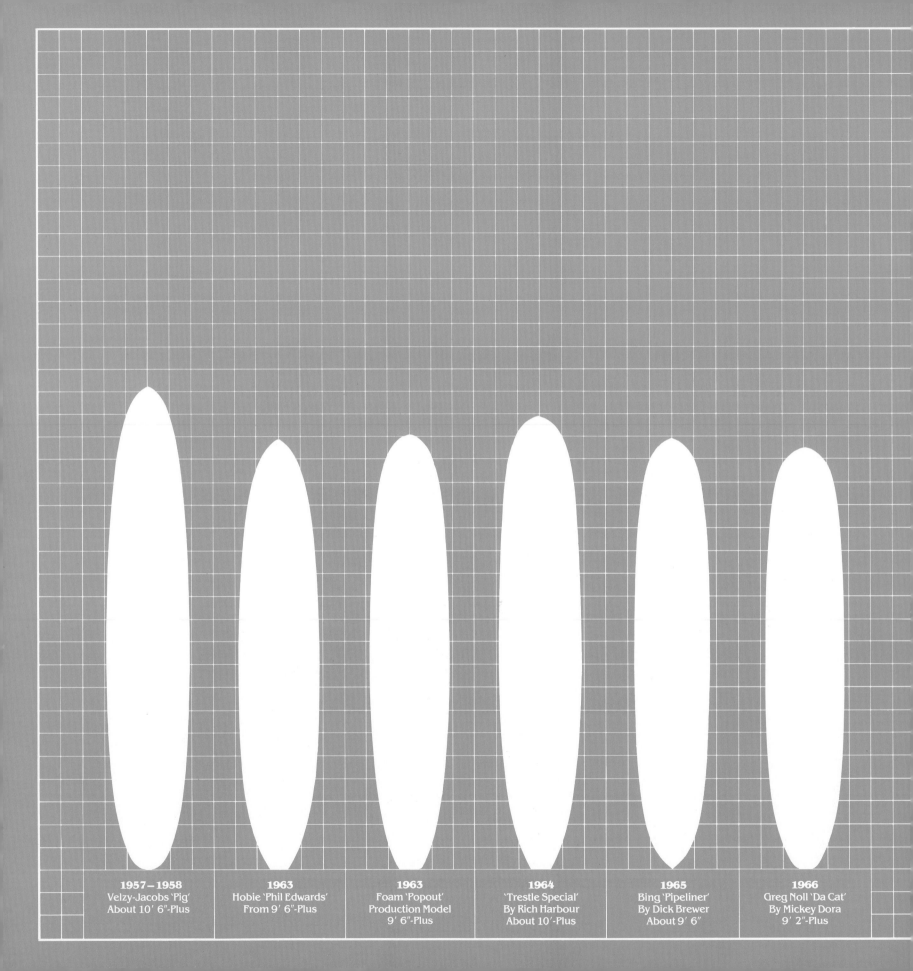

1957–1958
Velzy-Jacobs 'Pig'
About 10′ 6″-Plus

1963
Hobie 'Phil Edwards'
From 9′ 6″-Plus

1963
Foam 'Popout'
Production Model
9′ 6″-Plus

1964
'Trestle Special'
By Rich Harbour
About 10′-Plus

1965
Bing 'Pipeliner'
By Dick Brewer
About 9′ 6″

1966
Greg Noll 'Da Cat'
By Mickey Dora
9′ 2″-Plus

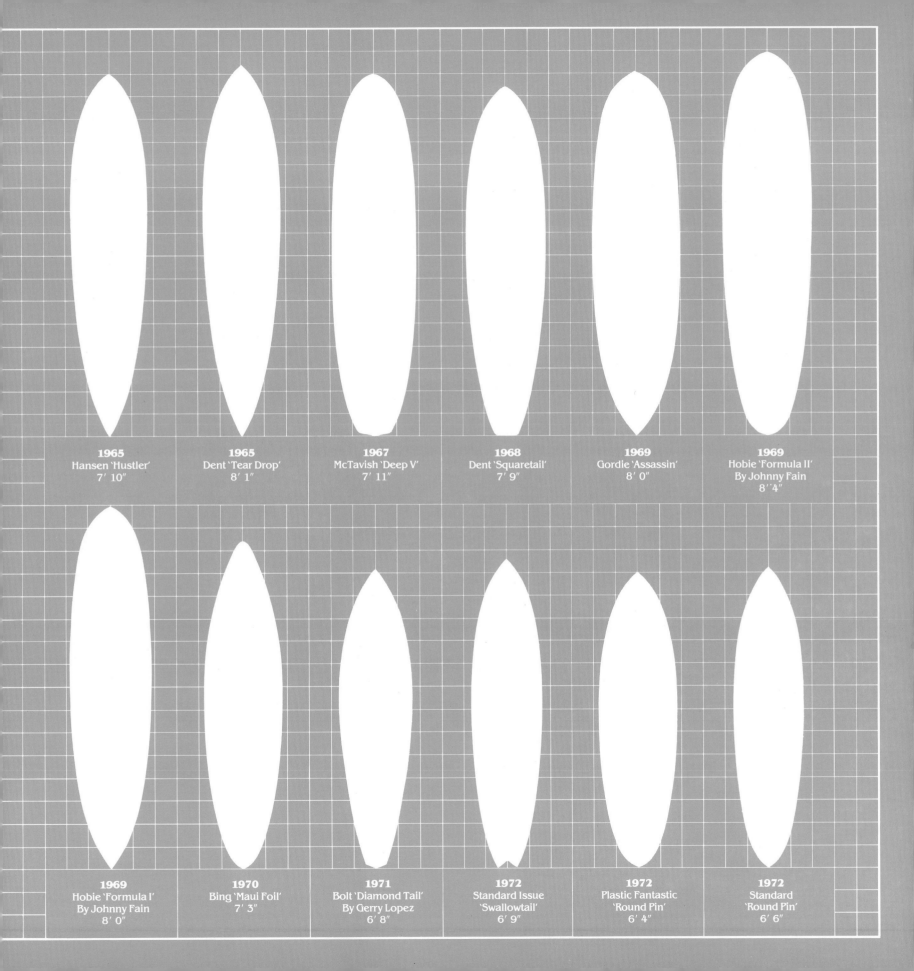

1965
Hansen 'Hustler'
7' 10"

1965
Dent 'Tear Drop'
8' 1"

1967
McTavish 'Deep V'
7' 11"

1968
Dent 'Squaretail'
7' 9"

1969
Gordie 'Assassin'
8' 0"

1969
Hobie 'Formula II'
By Johnny Fain
8' 4"

1969
Hobie 'Formula I'
By Johnny Fain
8' 0"

1970
Bing 'Maui Foil'
7' 3"

1971
Bolt 'Diamond Tail'
By Gerry Lopez
6' 8"

1972
Standard Issue
'Swallowtail'
6' 9"

1972
Plastic Fantastic
'Round Pin'
6' 4"

1972
Standard
'Round Pin'
6' 6"

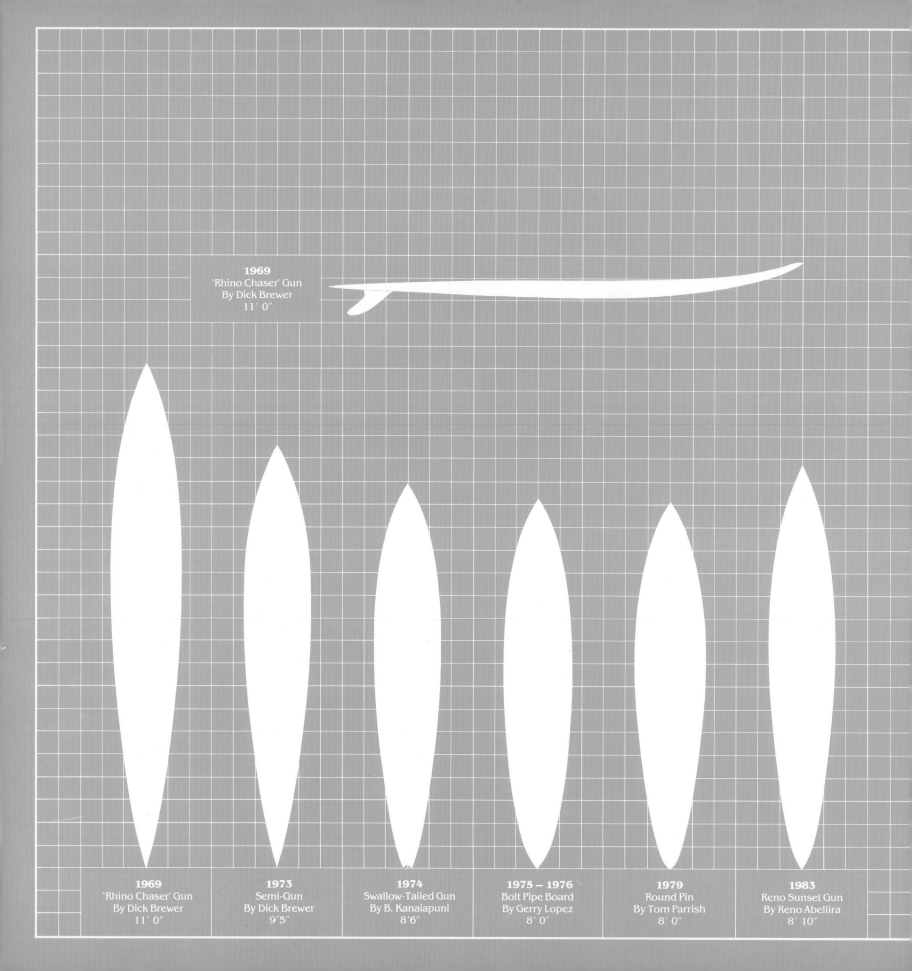

1969
'Rhino Chaser' Gun
By Dick Brewer
11' 0"

1969
'Rhino Chaser' Gun
By Dick Brewer
11' 0"

1973
Semi-Gun
By Dick Brewer
9'5"

1974
Swallow-Tailed Gun
By B. Kanaiapuni
8'6"

1975 — 1976
Bolt Pipe Board
By Gerry Lopez
8' 0"

1979
Round Pin
By Tom Parrish
8' 0"

1983
Reno Sunset Gun
By Reno Abellira
8' 10"

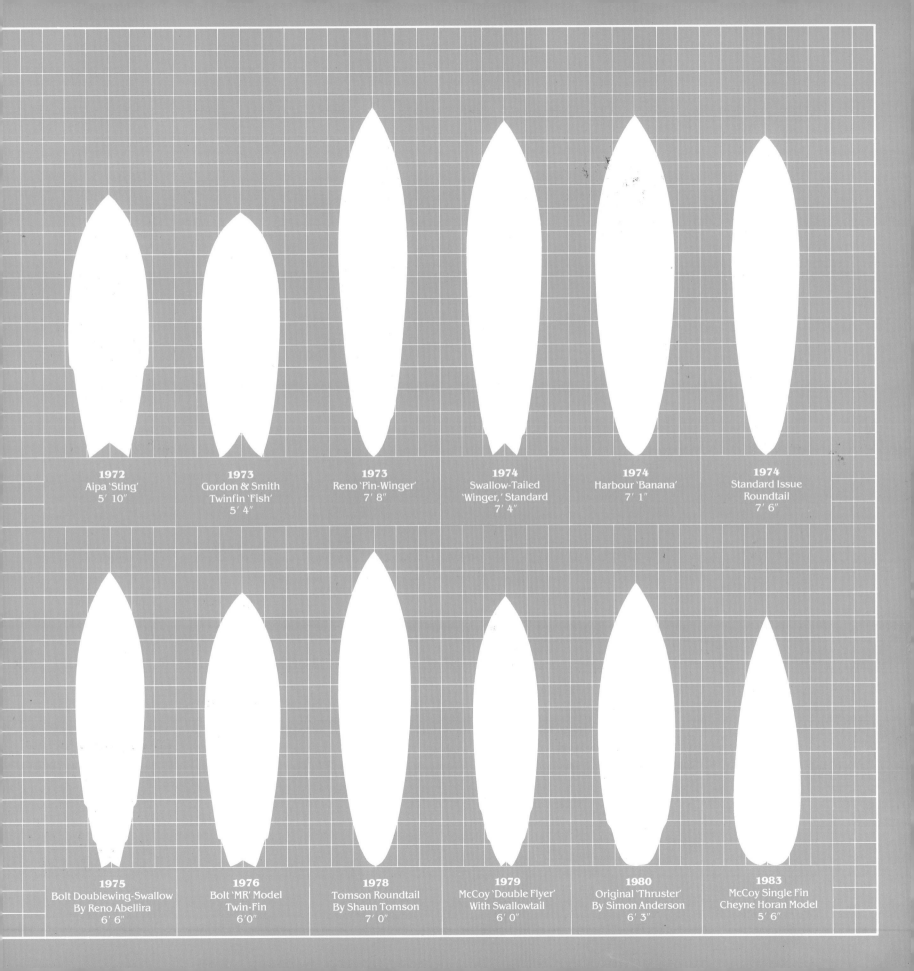

1972
Aipa 'Sting'
5' 10"

1973
Gordon & Smith
Twinfin 'Fish'
5' 4"

1973
Reno 'Pin-Winger'
7' 8"

1974
Swallow-Tailed
'Winger,' Standard
7' 4"

1974
Harbour 'Banana'
7' 1"

1974
Standard Issue
Roundtail
7' 6"

1975
Bolt Doublewing-Swallow
By Reno Abellira
6' 6"

1976
Bolt 'MR' Model
Twin-Fin
6' 0"

1978
Tomson Roundtail
By Shaun Tomson
7' 0"

1979
McCoy 'Double Flyer'
With Swallowtail
6' 0"

1980
Original 'Thruster'
By Simon Anderson
6' 3"

1983
McCoy Single Fin
Cheyne Horan Model
5' 6"

FRANKIE AVALON — muscle beach party AND OTHER MOTION PICTURE SONGS

MUSCLE BEACH PARTY
A BOY NEEDS A GIRL
SURFER'S HOLIDAY
RUNNING WILD
DON'T STOP NOW
BEACH PARTY
MORE
MOON RIVER
DAYS OF WINE AND ROSES
NEVERTHELESS
AGAIN
STOLEN HOURS

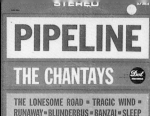

STEREO

PIPELINE

THE CHANTAYS

THE LONESOME ROAD • TRAGIC WIND •
RUNAWAY • BLUNDERBUS • BANZAI • SLEEP
WALK • • NIGHT THEME • • WAYWARD
NILE • EL CONQUISTADOR • RIDERS IN
THE SKY • • • LAST NIGHT • • • PIPELINE

SOUL SURFIN'
RHYTHM ROCKERS

SURF PUNKS

THE NO. 1 SURFING GROUP IN THE COUNTRY THE BEACH BOYS
SURFIN' USA

SURFIN' U.S.A • FARMER'S DAUGHTER • MISIRLOU • STOKED • LONELY SEA • SHUT DOWN
NOBLE SURFER • HONKY TONK • LANA • SURF JAM • LET'S GO TRIPPIN' • FINDERS KEEPERS

BOB VAUGHT & THE RENEGAIDS
SURF CRAZY

EXOTIC • SURFIN' TRAGEDY • MAKAHA • DELANO SOUL BEAT • LATINIA
TOR CHULA • BLUE MOON • MALIBU MASH • INTOXICA (SOUL) • RIN CON
REVELLION • SURFIN' SAFARI

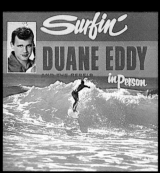

Surfin'
DUANE EDDY
AND THE REBELS
in Person

DICK DALE and his Del-Tones
GREATEST HITS

Surfin' with the Astronauts

BIG SURF! THE SENTINALS

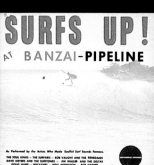

SURFS UP!
AT BANZAI-PIPELINE

As Performed by the Artists Who Made Soulful Surf Sounds Famous.
THE SOUL KINGS • THE SURFARIS • BOB VAUGHT AND THE RENEGADES
DAVE MYERS AND THE SURFTONES • JIM WALLER AND THE DELTAS
DOUG HUME • BISCAYNES • NEAL NISSENSON • BOB HAFNER

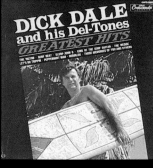

SURFER GIRL

including "MEMPHIS" & "SURFIN' USA"
CHUCK BERRY
CHESS LP 1480
ON STAGE

SURFIN' BIRD
KING OF SURF
THE TRASHMEN

BIRD IS THE WORD
THE SLEEPER
HONEY
TUBE CITY
MISIRLOU
MY WOODS
BOX
IT'S SO EASY
MALAGUENA
HENRIETTA

KFWB'S BATTLE OF
THE SURFING BANDS!

THE LIVELY ONES

MY SON THE SURF NUT

The following selected discography of surf music includes only long play albums. We have not included surf music 45 rpm singles due to space considerations.

Persons interested in more detailed surf music listings should consult periodic *Who Put The Bomp* catalogues issued by Bomp Records (P.O. Box 7112, Burbank, California 91510) or occasional discographies of surf music published by J. Bee Productions (John W. Blair, editor P.O. Box 1585, Riverside, California 92502).

Other good surf music sources include Carlos Hagen, a University of California at Los Angeles (UCLA) librarian who has produced "California Surf Music" documentaries for Los Angeles radio station KPFK, and Hollywood disc jockey Rodney Bingenheimer, who in recent years has produced several L.A.-KROQ radio shows that devote an inordinate amount of time to surf music and surf musicians.

Mike Adams & The Red Jackets
Surfer's Beat, Crown 312.
Adrian And The Sunsets
Breakthrough, Sunset 63-601.
Aki Aleong & The Nobles
Come Surf With Me, Vee-Jay LP-1060.
Davie Allan & The Arrows
Stoked on Surf!, What Records 601.
Richie Allen & The Pacific Surfers
Rising Surf, Imperial 9229.
Surfer's Slide, Imperial 9243.
Pua Almeida/Polynesians
Surfrider (& The Sport of Kings), Waikiki Records 314.
Astronauts (The)
Astronauts Orbit Campus, RCA 2903.
Competition Coupe, RCA 2858.

Down the Line, RCA 3454.
Everything is A-Okay, RCA 2782.
For You— From Us, RCA 3359.
Go . . . Go . . . Go!, RCA 3307.
Rockin' With The Astronauts, RCA PRM 183.
Surfin' With The Astronauts, RCA LPM/LSP 2760.
Travelin' Men, RCA 3733.
Avalanches
Ski Surfin', Warner Brothers 1525.
Frankie Avalon
Muscle Beach Party, United Artists 6371.

Beach Boys
Concert, Capitol (S)T-2198.
Surfer Girl, Capitol (S)T-1981.
Surfin' Safari, Capitol (S)T-1808.
Surfin' USA, Capitol (S)T-1890.
& Jan and Dean, Exact 243.
plus many more
Blasters
Sound of the Drags, Crown 392.
Chuck Berry
Onstage, Chess LP1480.
Bongo Teens
Surfin' Bongos, Original Sound 5009/S-8872.
Buddies
Go-Go, Wing 16306.
& Comets, Wing 16293.

Al Casey
Surfin' Hootenanny, Stacy 100.
Catalinas
Fun Fun Fun, Ric 1006.
Centurions
Surfer's Pajama Party, Del-Fi DFST/ DFLP-1228.
Challengers (The)
At The Teenage Fair, GNP Crescendo 2010.
& Billy Strange, GNP 2030.
California Kicks, GNP 2025.
Challengers A Go-Go, Vault 110.
The Challengers Go Sidewalk Surfin', Triumph 100.
Go Sidewalk Surfin', Triumph 100.
Greatest Hits, GNP 609.
K-39, Vault Records, Inc. 107.

Light My Fire With Classical Gas, GNP 2045.
The Man From U.N.C.L.E., GNP 2018.
Surfbeat, Vault 100.
Surfing Around the World, Vault 102.
Surfing With The Challengers, Vault 101A.
Surf's Up (The Challengers on TV), Vault 111.
Vanilla Funk, GNP 2056.
Where Were YOU in the Summer of '62, Fantasy 9443.
Wipeout, GNP Crescendo 2031.
Chantays
Pipeline, Downey 1002.
Two Sides of the Chantays, Dot DLP-3771/25771.
Jerry Cole & His Spacemen
Hot Rod Dance Party, Capitol (S)T-2061.
Outer Limits, Capitol (S)T-2044.
Surf Age, Capitol (S)T-2112.
Competitors
Little Deuce Coupe /409, Dot 25542.
Calvin Cool & The Surf Knobs
The Surfer's Beat, Charter CL/CLS-103.
Cornells (The)
Beach Bound, Garex LPGA-100.

Don Dailey
Surf Stompin', Crown 5314/ CST-314.
Dick Dale & His Deltones
Checkered Flag, Capitol (S)T-2002.
King of the Surf Guitars, Capitol (S)T-1930.
Summer Surf, Capitol (S)T-2111.
Surfer's Choice, Deltone LPM-1001.
Surfer's Choice, Deltone T/DT-1886.
Greatest Hits, GNP Crescendo GNPS-2095.

Darts
Hollywood Drag, Del-Fi 1244.
Deadly Ones
Its Monster Surfing Time, Vee-Jay VLP-1090.
De-Fenders
De-Fenders Play the Big Ones, World Pacific 1810.
Drag Beat, Del-Fi 1242.
Deuce Coupes
Hotrodders' Choice, Del-Fi 1243.
The Shut Downs, Crown 393.
Bo Diddley
Surfin' With Bo Diddley, Checker 2987.
Mike Doyle
Secrets of Surfing, Fleetwood FLP-3018.
Duals
Stick Shift, Sue 2002.

Duane Eddy
Surfin', Jamie JLP-3024.
Preston Epps
Surfin' Bongos, Original Sound 5009/8872.

Fantastic Baggys
Surf Craze, Import (Edsel)
Tell 'Em I'm Surfin', Imperial 9270/12270.
Fireballs
Here are the Fireballs, Warwick 2042.
Torquay, DOT DLP-3512/25512.
Johnny Fortune
The Soul Surfer, Park Ave. 401/1301.
Annette Funicello
Annette's Beach Party, Buena Vista BV-3316.
Muscle Beach Party, Buena Vista BV-3314.
Sings Golden Surfin' Hits, Buena Vista BV-3327.

Ghouls
Dracula's Deuce, Capitol 2215.
Glaciers
From Sea to Ski, Mercury MG 20895/SR-60895
Good Guys
Side Walk Surfing, GNP Crescendo 2001.
Guitar Ramblers
Happy, Youthful New Sounds of . . ., Columbia Cl-2067.

Jimmie Haskell
Sunset Surf, Capitol (S)T-1915.
Hondells
Go Little Honda, Mercury 20940.
The Hondells, Mercury.
Hornets
Big Drag Boats U.S.A., Liberty 7364.
Motorcycles U.S.A., Liberty 7348.
Hot Doggers
Hot Doggers, Epic LN-24054/BN-26054.
Hot Rodders
Big Hot Rod, Crown 378.
Joe Houston
Surf Rockin', Crown 5313/CST-313.

Impacts (The)
Wipeout, Del-Fi DFLP/DFST-1234.

Jan and Dean
Command Performance, Liberty LRP-3403/LST-7403.
Drag City, Liberty LRP-3389/LST-7389.
Jan and Dean With the Soul Surfers, L-J 101.
Little Old Lady From Pasadena, Liberty LRP 3377/LST-7377.
Ride the Wild Surf, Liberty LRP-3368/LS 7368.
Surf City, Liberty LRP-3314/LST-7314.
Take Linda Surfin', Liberty LRP-3294/LST-7294.
Bruce Johnston Surfing Band
Surfer's Pajama Party, Del-Fi DFLP/DFST 1228.
Surfin' Round the World, Columbia CL-2057/CS-8857.

Kickstands
Black Boots & Bikes, Capitol 2078.
Knights
Hot Rod High, Capitol 2189.
Jerry Kole & Strokers
Hot Rod Alley, Crown 5385.
Kustom Kings
Kustom City U.S.A., Smash MGS-27051/SRS-67051.

Lively Ones (The)
Surf City, Del-Fi DFLP/DFST-1237.
Surf Drums, Del-Fi DFLP/DFST-1231.

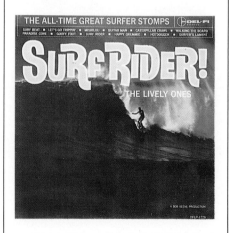

Surf Rider, Del-Fi DFLP/DFST-1226.
The Great Surf Hits, Del-Fi DFLP/
DFST-1238.

Lively Ones & Surf Mariachis
Surfin' South of the Border, Del-Fi
1240.

Malibooz
Malibooz Rule, Rhino 100.

Marketts
Out of Limits, Warner Brothers
1537.
Sun Power, Warner Brothers 1870.
Surfer's Stomp, Liberty LRP-3226/
LST-7226.
The Marketts Take to Wheels,
Warner Brothers 1709.
The Surfing Scene, Liberty LRP-
3226/LST-7226.

Jim Messina & The Jesters
Jim Messina & The Jesters, Thim-
ble TLP-3. (1973 reissue)
The Dragsters, Audio Fidelity DFM-
3037/DFS-7037.

Mixtures (The)
Stompin' At The Rainbow, Linda
3301.

Vaughn Monroe
Surfer's Stomp, Dot DLP-2419/
25419.

Mr. Gasser & Weirdos
Hot Rod Hootenanny, Capitol
2010.
Rod n' Ratfinks, Capitol 2057.
Sufink! Capitol 2114.

Mustangs
Dartell Stomp, Providence 001.

Dave Myers & The Surftones
Hangin' Twenty, Del-Fi DFLP/DFST-
1239.

Dave Myers Effect
Greatest Racing Themes, Carole
8002.

Neptunes
Surfer's Holiday, Family 552.

New Dimensions
Deuces and Eights, Sutton 331.
Soul Surf, Sutton 336.
Surf 'N Bongos, Sutton 332.

Jack Nitzsche
The Lonely Surfer, Reprise R(S)-
6101.

Nobles (The)
Come Surf With Me, Vee-Jay VLP-
1060.

Packards (The)
Pray for Surf, Surfside 001 Stereo.

Persuaders
Surfer's Nightmare, Saturn 5000.

Pyramids (The)
Penetration And Other Favorites,
Best BR-16501/BRS-36501.

Revels (The)
The Revels on a Rampage,
Impact 1.

Rhythm Rockers
Soul Surfin', Challenge CH-617.
Sun Rockabillies, Vol. 1. Sun 1010.

Rincon Surfside Band
The Surfing Songbook, Dunhill
D(S)-50001

Rip Chords
California U.S.A., Columbia C2-
37412.
Hey Little Cobra, Columbia 8951.
Three Window Coupe, Columbia

CL-2216/CS-8916.

Risers
She's a Bad Motorcycle, Imperial
9269.

Rivieras
California Sun, USA 102.
Campus Party, Riviera 701.

Road Runners
The New Mustang, London 5381.

Rod & The Cobras
Drag Race at Surf City, Somerset
SF-20500.

Ronny & The Daytones
GTO, Mala 4001.
Sandy, Mala 4002.

Routers
Let's Go, Warner Brothers 1490.
1963's Great Instrumental Hits,
Warner Brothers 1524.
Play the Chuck Berry Songbook,
Warner Brothers 1595.
Super Bird, Mercury 682.

Rumblers
Boss! Downey DLP-1001.

Sandals (The)
The Endless Summer, World Pacific
1832.

Satans
Raisin' Hell, no label.

Scramblers
Cycle Psychos, Crown 5384.
Little Honda, Wyncote 9048.

Sentinals
Big Surf, Del-Fi DFLP/DFST-1232.
Surfer Girl, Del-Fi DFLP/DFST-
1241.
Vegas Go Go, Sutton (S) SU-338.

John Severson
Sunset Surf, Capitol 1915.

Shadows
Surfing With The Shadows, Atlantic
8089.

Silly Surfers
Sounds of the Silly Surfers,
Mercury 60977.

Spinners
 Party— My Pad After Surfin', Time 52092.
Squiddly Diddly
 Surfin' Surfari, HBR 2043.
Sunrays
 Andrea, Tower 5017.
Sunsets
 Surfin' With The Sunsets, Palace 752.
Super Stocks
 School is a Drag, Capitol 2190.
 Surf Route 101, Capitol (S)T-2113.
 Thunder Road, Capitol 2060.
Surf Knobs
 Surfer's Beat, Charter 103.
Surf Riders
 Surf Beat, Vault 105.
Surf Punks
 My Beach, Epic NJE-36500.
Surf Stompers
 Original Surfer Stomp, Del-Fi DFLP/ DFST-1236.
Surf Teens
 Surf Mania, Sutton (S) SU-339.
Surfaris (The)
 Fun City USA, Decca DL-4560/ 74560
 Hit City, '64, Decca DL-4487/ 74487.
 Hit City, '65, Decca DL-4614/ 74614.
 It Ain't Me Babe, Decca 4683.
 Play, Decca 4470.
 The Surfaris, Decca DL-4470/ 74470.
 Wheels, Diplomat 2309.
 Wipeout, Dot DLP-3535/25535.
Surfing Seminar
 with Joey Cabell, Del Cannon, Mike Doyle, Joyce Hoffman, Chuck Linnen, Mickey Munoz.

T-Bones
 Boss Drag, Liberty 7346
 Boss Drag at the Beach, Liberty 7363.

Tides
 Surf City and Other Favorites, Wing MGW-12265.
Tokens
 Wheels, RCA 2886.
Tom And Jerry
 Surfin' Hootenanny, Mercury MG-20842/SR-60842.
Tornadoes (The)
 Bustin' Surfboards, Josie 4005.
Torques
 Zoom, (local label, Princeton, NJ).
Trashmen
 Surfin' Bird, Garrett LPGA-200.

V.A.
 Shut Downs and Hill Climbs, Liberty 7365.
Ricky Vale & His Surfers
 Everybody's Surfin', Strand SL(S)-1104.
Bob Vaught & The Renegaids
 Surf Crazy, GNP Crescendo 83.
Ventures (The)
 Beach Party, Dolton BLP-2016/ BST-8016.
 Surfing, Dolton BLP-2022/BST-8022.
Vettes
 Rev-Up, MGM E/SE-4193

Jim Waller & The Deltas
 Surfin' Wild, Arvee A-432.
Wave Crests
 Surftime U.S.A., Viking 6606.

Wedges
 Hang Ten, Time 52090/S-2090
Weird-Ohs
 Sounds of the Silly Surfers, Mercury MG-20977/SR-60977.
Burt Wheels & Speedsters
 Sounds of the Big Racers, Coronet 216.
Willie & The Wheels
 Surfin' Songbook, RCA 70044.
Kai Winding
 Soul Surfin', Verve 8551.
Winners
 Checkered Flag, Crown 5394.
Woofers
 Dragsville, Wyncote 9011.

Neil Young
 Surfer Joe and Moe the Sleaze, RPS 50014.

Zip-Codes
 Mustang!, Liberty 3367.

MULTIPLE ARTIST LISTINGS

Almor
The World of Surfin', Dick Dale, Fireballs, Surf Teens, and The Surfaris, Almor 108.

Ava
Surf Party, Surfaris et. al. AVA 28.

Capitol
Chartbusters, Beach Boys et. al., Capitol (S)T-1837.
Chartbusters, Vol. 2, Beach Boys et. al., Capitol (S)T-1945.
Chartbusters, Vol. 3, Beach Boys et. al., Capitol (S)T-2006.
Exciting New Releases, featuring Dick Dale and The Beach Boys, Capitol PRO-2376.
Hot Rod Rally, Roger Christian, Steve Douglas, Super Stocks, Capitol 1997.
My Son the Surf Nut, featuring the Newport Little Theatre Surfing Group, Capitol (S)T-1939.

Del-Fi
Battle of the Surfing Bands, Biscaynes and The Charades, The Challengers, Impacts, Bruce Johnston, Lively Ones, Dave Myers and the Surftones, Rhythm Kings, Sentinals, Soul Kings, Jim Waller & The Deltas, Del-Fi DFLP/DFST-1235/

Diplomat
Dick Dale With Bo Troy & His Hot Rods, same artists, D-2304.

Dubtone
Dick Dale and The Hollywood Surfers, same artists, Dubtone LP-1246.

GNP Crescendo
Original Surfin' Hits, The Breakers, Dave Myers & The Surftones, Rhythm Kings, Sentinals, Soul Kings, Jim Waller & The Deltas, Bob Vaught & The Renegaids, GNP 84.
Surf Battle, Dave Myers & The Surftones, Rhythm Kings, GNP 85.

GSP
George Sherwood Presents, Breakers, Charades, Kenny & The Sultans, Dave Kinzie, Gary Paxton, Revels,

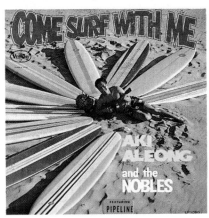

Judy Russell, Sandford & The Sandies, Sentinals, Surfaris, Surf Bunnies, GSP 6901.

Guest Star
Surf Kings, The Beach Boys, Dick Dale, Guest Star, Surfaris, The Surf Kings, G-1433.

Impact
Shake, Shout, and Soul, Steve Korey, Lil' Ray, Daye Myers & The Surftones, New Dimensions, Surfaris, The Virtue 4, Impact 2.

King
Look Who's Surfin' Now, James Brown, King Curtis, Tonni Kalash, Albert King, Freddy King, King Surfers, Little Willie John, Hank Moore, Johnny Otis, Gene Redd, The Surf Jumpers, Wild Kats. King 882.
Surfin' on Wave Nine, King 855.

Modern Sound
Draggin' and Surfin', Modern Sound 536.

Northridge
Surf's Up at Banzai Pipeline. Biscaynes, Bob Hafner, Doug Hume, Dave Myers & The Surftones, Neal Nissenson, Soul Kings, Surfaris, Bob Vaught & The Renegaids, Jim Waller & The Deltas, Northridge 101.

Reprise
Surf's Up at Banzai Pipeline, Same as on Northridge with more from The Surfaris and The Coast Continentals, Reprise 6094.

Rhino
History of Surf Music, Vol. 2. with Trashmen, Turtles, and others. RHI 052.
History of Surf Music, Vol. 3. with Evasions, Malibooz, Surf Punks, Surf Raiders and others. RHI 054.

Shepherd
Surf War— The Battle of the Surf Groups, Centurians, The Impacts, Dave Myers & The Surftones, Bob Vaught & The Renegaids, Jim Waller & The Deltas, Sheperd 1300.

Star
Battle of the Bands, Adventures, Arcades, Checkmates, Dimensions, Duplex, Escorts, Frolic Five, Impacts, The Infusions, Kona Casuals, Lepricons, Majestics, Raiders, Renegaids, Rivals, Royal Malads, Sensations, Star Lighters, Statics, Thunderbird, Star 101.

Vault
Hot Rod City, The Customs, The Grand Prix, Quads, Vault 104. Oldies, Goodies, and Woodies, Beach Girls, Busy Bodies, The Challengers, Gladiators, Tom Starr & The Galaxies, Vibrents, Vault 103.

A SURF FILMOGRAPHY

With Diamond Head as a backdrop, an early moviemaker, Robert A. Bonine, captures early surfing action on the beach at world-famous Waikiki.

The following selected filmography includes — in chronological order — the titles and producers of films, both educational and commercial, that are about or include significant or curious information about surfing. Because of the "underground" nature of many so-called "surf films," it was impossible to compile a truly complete listing of this film genre as of this printing.

The publisher would like to improve on our current listing of films in future editions of this book, so we would like to invite interested parties to please send us the names, producers and dates of release of any surf films that may have been inadvertently omitted. Address such data to: Emphasis International, 832 Halekauwila Street, Honolulu, Hawaii 96813 U.S.A.

1898
Thomas Edison films surfers at Waikiki.

1943
The Big Surf, Bud Browne, USA.

1945
Hawaiian Memories, Bud Browne, USA.

1953
Hawaiian Surfing Movies, Bud Browne, USA.

1954
Hawaiian Holiday, Bud Browne, USA.

1955
Hawaiian Surfing Movies, Bud Browne, USA.

1956
Hawaii, Island of Dreams, Trek to Makaha, Bud Browne, USA.

1957
The Big Surf, Bud Browne, USA.

1958
Slippery When Wet, Bruce Brown, U.S.A. Island surf and a soundtrack by altoist Bud Shank.
Surf Down Under, Bud Browne, USA. The first international surf movie.

1959
Cat on a Hot Foam Board, Bud Browne, USA.
Gidget, Columbia Pictures, USA. At Malibu with "the little girl with big ideas." Starring Sandra Dee and Mickey Munoz (in bikini and wig).

1960
Sacrifice Surf, Bob Bagley, USA. Big surf and surfing sacrifices.
Surf Fever, John Severson, USA.
Surf Happy, Bud Browne, USA.
Surf Trek to Hawaii, Bob Evans, Australia. Featuring Bernard "Midget" Farrelly.

1961
Gidget Goes Hawaiian, Jerry Bresler Productions, USA. Gidget and Jeff's relationship gets complicated on the beach at Waikiki.
Midget Goes Hawaiian, Bob Evans, Australia. Evans takes young Midget Farrelly to the Islands.
Spinning Boards, Bud Browne, USA.

1962
Cavalcade of Surf, Bud Browne, USA.
Going My Wave, John Severson, USA.
Psyche Out, Walt Phillips, USA.
Surfing Hollow Days, Bruce Brown, USA.
Surfing in Hawaii, Clarence Maki, USA.
Surfing the Southern Cross, Bob Evans, Australia. Another look at Down Under's Midget.

1963
Beach Party. Alta Vista Productions, USA. Frankie Avalon takes his girl to a secluded beach house for surf and romance only to find their friends are already there.
Gun Ho, Bud Browne, USA.
Have Board Will Travel, Don Brown, USA.
Hawaiian Thrills, Bob Evans, Australia.
Northside Story, Val Valentine, USA. Great surf on Oahu's North Shore.
North Swell, Grant Rohloff, USA.

1964
Always Another Wave, Don Wolf, USA. A historic look at surfing, with Rick Grigg and Mickey Munoz.
The Call of the Surf, Val Valentine, USA. Hawaii: Makaha, Waikiki, Laniakea and Yokohama.
Gone With The Wave, Phil Wilson, USA.
Let There Be Surf, Jim Freeman, USA.
Locked In, Bud Browne, USA.
Muscle Beach Party, Alta Vista Productions, USA. Muscle men invade the surfers' territory, starring Mickey Dora, Johnny Fain, and Little Stevie Wonder.
Outside the Third Dimension. Jim Freeman, USA. The only 3-D surf movie.
Ride on the Wild Side, Ed De Priest, USA.
Ride the Wild Surf, Jana Film Enterprises, USA. This classic beach movie sets romance and macho competition on the stage of big Waimea.
Strictly Hot, Dale Davis, USA.
Surf Classics, John Severson, USA. Highlights from 11 years of Severson's footage.
The Waves, Walt Philips, USA. Malibu, Hawaii, Huntington.
The Young Wave Hunters, Bob Evans, Australia. Stalking waves with Nat Young (and others) on Australia's east coast.

1965

A Cool Wave of Color, Greg MacGillivray, USA. Good California hot-dogging.

Beach Ball, The Patton Company, USA. The Wiggles, a rock n' roll band, drop out of show biz to enjoy Malibu beach life.

Beach Blanket Bingo, American International, USA. Frankie and Dee Dee take up skydiving.

The Beach Girls and The Monster, American Academy Productions. Surfer Mark is being seduced by his friend's step-mother when they are interrupted by a sea monster.

Dr. Strangesurf, Walt Phillips, USA.

Long Way 'Round, Bob Evans, Australia. Including Peru waves.

The Performers, Greg MacGillivray, USA. Richard Chew and Bob Limacher surf Hawaii, Baja, Florida, Mexico, and California.

Some Like it Wet, Brad Page, USA.

Stop the Wave, I Want to Get Off, Jim Wilhoite, USA. Mickey Munoz and Butch Van Artsdalen on Maui.

Surfing Aussie, Val Valentine, USA. Shown only a few times on Oahu.

Surfing Roundabout, David Price, Australia. Narrated with wit by Richard Neville.

Walk on the Wet Side, Dale Davis, USA.

1966

A Life in the Sun, Paul Witzig, Australia. Queensland curls.

A Place Called Malibu, Dale Davis, USA.

Another Wave, Barry Mirandon, David Kay, USA.

Boardriders, Bill Fitzwater, Australia. Score by Vivaldi; for ABC-TV.

The Endless Summer, Bruce Brown, USA. For much of the world, this is still THE surf movie. Mike Hynson and Robert August search the world for the perfect wave.

Don Brown presents..
His 1963 Intenational SURF Adventure Color Movie
"Have Board Will Travel"

Filmed in
****
• Australia
• Hawaii
• California
• Mexico
• Brazil & Peru

John Muir High School
1905 Lincoln Avenue - Pasadena
8 P.M. **Friday, March 22**
Open to Public   Tickets at door $1.25

High on a Cool Wave, Bob Evans, Australia. Featuring Bob McTavish.

Inside Out, Dale Davis, USA.

Surf Crazy, Bruce Brown, USA.

The Surfing Years, Peter Thompson, Australia. An ABC-TV documentary.

1967

Don't Make Waves, Filmways, Inc, USA. Tony Curtis and Sharon Tate star; based on Ira Wallach's book, **Muscle Beach.**

Eden Cried, 4028 Productions, USA.

The Hot Generation, Paul Witzig, Australia. A who's who of Aussie waveriders.

Mondo Mod, Timely Motion Pictures, USA. Surfing is featured in a look at leisure activities of American youth.

Ride a White Horse, Bob Evans, Australia. Re-runs.

The Way We Like It, Bob Evans, Australia. Introducing Tanya Binning.

World Champion Wavemen, Bob Evans, Australia. Yet more recycled wave footage.

1968

Free and Easy, MacGillivray and Freeman, USA.

The Golden Breed, Dale Davis, USA. Joey Cabell, Jock Sutherland, Nat Young, and Felipe Pomar on another quest for perfect surf in Hawaii, Mexico, and California.

Splashdown, Bob Evans, Australia.

1969

Evolution, Paul Witzig, Australia. Wayne Lynch and Nat Young push the limits.

The Fantastic Plastic Machine, Eric and Lowell Blum, 1969. After Nat Young wins the World Championships in San Diego, The Wind and Sea Surf Club goes to Australia, looking for a rematch. They discover the "short-board."

Fluid Journey, DES Films, USA. Poor quality.

Follow Me, Robert Peterson, USA. East Coast surfers Claude Codgen and Bub Purvey surf Morocco, Ceylon, India, Japan, and Hawaii.

For Those Who Think Young, Schenk-Koch, USA. Grandfathers and cranky professors get in the way of some students who want some good, clean fun.

The Living Curl, Jamie Budge, USA. Not the best California surf.

Who's Best, MacGillivray and Freeman, USA. A fifteen minute short comparing Nuhuuiwa, Corky Carrol, Wayne Lynch, and Nat Young.

1970

The Cosmic Children, Hal Jepson. Strong footage of J. Riddle, Rolf Arness in California; Barry Kanaiaupuni and Jeff Hakman carving big Sunset.

Freedom, Rodney Sumpter, Great Britain. Rodney Sumpter surfing tidal bores.

Getting Back to Nothing, Tim Burstall, Australia. Nitty-gritty TV documentary of the 1970 Australian Nationals.

The Innermost Limits of Pure Fun. George Greenough. Timeless, slow motion views from deep in the tube.

The Natural Art, Fred Windisch. Psychedelic soul surfing: lots of visual effects; 1968 World Contest in Puerto Rico.

Pacific Vibrations, John Severson. Beautiful footage of Jock Sutherland flowing around and through big Hono Wa's tubes; strong statement of surfing as a peaceful lifestyle.

Seaweed Sandwich, Merrill-Hammond Productions. Hollywood documentary of beach life in San Diego.

Splashdown, Bob Evans, Australia. 1970 World Contest; Terry Fitzgerald ripping Narrabeen.

Total Involvement. Bill Kaiwa. Hardly seen outside Hawaii. Reno Abellira and Gerry Lopez display the creativity which signalled their future greatness.

Tracks, Bob Evans, Australia.

Waves of Change, MacGillivray and Freeman. Innovative water angles and innovative surfing from Keith Paull, Bill Hamilton, and Mark Martinson in Europe.

1971

Animals, Paul Witzig, Australia.

Family Free, Bob Evans, Australia. On Aussie's east and west coasts.

Oceans, Rodney Sumpter, Great Britain. Brad McCaul in huge Jeffrey's Bay, Rory Russell at Pipeline.

Rainbow Bridge, Anpahkarana Productions, USA. Featuring Jimi Hendrix on Maui.

Sea of Joy, Paul Witzig, Australia.

Seadreams, Curt Mastalka and Peter French, USA. Rory Russell, Randy Becht, and Bill Lacy, the hottest kids in Hawaii at the time.

The Sunshine Sea, McGillivray and Freeman, USA. **Waves of Change**

updated and blown up to 35mm for general release.

1972

Directions, Bruce Walker, USA. Super-8 of good Florida and Huntington Pier.

Expression Session II, Hal Jepson. Thoughtfully edited documentary of the second Expression Session. Surfer's styles are compared with each other at Pipeline and Sunset.

Five Summer Stories, McGillivray and Freeman, USA. One of the very best. Bud Browne's water photography at Pipeline set the standard for every movie that followed.

In Natural Flow, Steve Core, Australia. Beautiful Kirra from the water.

The Islands, Paul Witzig, Australia.

Island Magic, John Hitchcock, USA. Hawaii: inside look at the Neighbor Islands, with Jim Lucas and Joey Cabell out in beautiful, green Hanalei

Bay, and a hilarious interview with Owl Chapman and Dick Brewer.

Morning of the Earth, Albert Falzon, Australia. Bali, Hawaii and Down Under.

Nirvanic Symphony, Murray McIntosh. France and Hawaii with Jeff Hakman.

Our Day in the Sun, Sheppard and Usher, Australia.

Surfing Odyssey, John Phillips, Australia. Coverage of this year's Smirnoff contest in Hawaii for the C-10 TV group.

Zephyr, Yuri Farrant, USA. Grassroots Hawaiian surfing. The water photography at Waimea shows the size and mass of the surf.

1973

A Winter's Tale, Sheppard and Usher, Australia. Lots of good, hollow Australian point surf with Michael Peterson, Simon Anderson.

Better Days, Jim Clark, USA. Super 8 of Hawaii and California.

Cold Lines, Paul Gillane and Greg Huglin, USA. Super 8 of California between Santa Barbara and San Francisco with a taste of Hawaii.

Crystal Voyager, Albert Falzon and George Greenough, Australia. A profile of George Greenough; music by Pink Floyd.

Echos, George Greenough. Views from inside the tube looking out and outside the tube looking in.

Goin Surfin', Bud Browne, USA. Superb editing and pacing, many truly funny moments, and Dora and Edwards surfing to Dave Brubeck.

In Natural Flow, Steve Core, Australia.

Inspiration, Larry Bennet, USA. George Greenough tube-riding a long, deep California point and Larry Bertlemann ripping Ventura.

Summer Breeze, Allen Maine, USA. Great hot-dogging. Larry Bertlemann in San Diego; Gerry Lopez carving Ala Moana along with Michael Ho.

Waves Seen, Paul Gross, Australia. An Australian's view of California.

1974

A Fluid Drive, Scott Dittrich and Skip Smith, USA. Hard-core, rock n' roll presentation of surfing as a primal drive. Great footage of Bill Hamilton's mature and polished surfing.

Drouyn, Bob Evans, Australia. Bob Evans takes surf-star Peter Drouyn around the world.

Forgotten Islands of Santosha, Larry Yates, USA. A quiet and philosophical film built around the long lefts of Mauritius. Joey Cabell's surfing there is precise, graceful, and totally controlled — one of surfing's great moments.

Liquid Space, Dale Davis, USA. Davis' first film in many years; good Pipeline and Sunset from a lackluster winter on the North Shore.

On Any Morning, David Sumpter, Australia. Waves and send-ups.

Rolling Home, Paul Witzig, Australia. Witzig documents the laid back, country side of Australian surfing.

Salt Water Wine, Alan Rich, USA. Sam Hawk dives around the Pipeline reef, talks about getting stuffed into the caves there, then rips it. Good Malibu with Hawaiians Reno Abellira and Ben Aipa.

Surfabout, Albert Falzon, Australia. A 35mm short report on the 1974 Coca Cola championship meet.

The Sun Seekers, Cording and Humphries, USA. Winner of the religious film category at the Atlanta Film Festival.

1975

Super Session, Hal Jepson, USA. Interviews with Lopez, Hakman, Russell, BK, and Bertlemann. Good sequences of Michael Peterson ripping Gold Coast point surf.

Tales from the Tube, Cording and Humphries, USA. Strong Pipeline, Rocky Point and V-Land and a philosophical, Christian view of life.

Waves, Gene Bagley and Bill Gellatly. USA.

1976

A Matter of Style, Steve Soderberg, USA. Great surfing; an attempt to compare styles of Lopez, Tomson, Fitzgerald, and others.

Cycles of the Northern Sun, Chris Klopf, USA. Lots of strong surfing from Northern California's secret spots.

Five Summer Stories Plus Four, MacGillivray and Freeman, USA.

Free Rides, Bruce Walker, USA. Lots of Florida surf with surprising footage of Miami Beach.

Harmony Within, Doug Swenson and Paul Dunaway, USA. Surfing as yoga. Lots of Mexico.

Hot Lips and Inner Tubes, Yuri Farrant, USA. Lopez at Uluwatu, and Hakman and Abellira at Maalaea.

Motion, Fowler Brothers, USA. An interesting assortment of motion sports, from hang-gliding to jet skis, and motor bikes in ice rinks, to surfing huge Honolua Bay.

Out of the Blue, Aaron Chang, USA. Super-8; good water photography of Hawaii.

Playgrounds in Paradise, Alan Rich. Great footage from a year's worth of good surf around the world.

Visions, Steve Bissel, USA. Central America and California, (slide-show).

1977

Ahoo!, Warner Wacha.

In Search of Tubular Swells, Dick Hoole and Jack McCoy. Straight ahead surfing, including one of the longest, most beautifully controlled tube-rides on film: Lopez, super-late into a lime green Uluwatu barrel.

In the Mist of Summer, Rick Jorgenson and Gary Pennington. Features Russell Short riding Bonzers in Mexico with Dan Flecky.

Room to Move I, Chris Bystrom, USA. Super 8 of California featuring 1977 Katin-Pro Am Team Challenge and Big Rock in San Diego.

1978

Big Wednesday, John Milius, USA. The great summer of 1963 at Malibu. Featuring Jan Michael-Vincent.

California Dreaming, directed by John Hancock, USA. Hollywood view of surfers as low lifes.

Free Ride, Bill Delaney, USA. Good water photography at Off The Wall of Wayne Bartholemew and Shaun Tomson. The profile of Bartholemew works better than most.

Hawaiian Safari, Rodney Sumpter, Great Britain.

Many Classic Moments, Gary Capo, USA. One of the best soundtracks ever, featuring Hawaii's Kalapana. Buttons Kaluhiokalani, Mark Liddell, and Dane Kealoha surf beautifully in small Hawaiian waves.

Room to Move II, C. Bystrom, USA.
SRO, Allen Main and Hugh Thomas, USA.
Style Masters, Greg Weaver, USA. Good, strong 8mm footage studies the styles of Mark Richards, Buttons, Mike Ho and others.
Wave Masters, Grant Young, Australia. Documents the 1978 Australian Pro Circuit. A short, called "Passing Images," features photographers Peter Crawford, Bruce Channon, John Ware, and Hugh McLeod.

1979
Apocalypse Now, Francis Ford Coppola, USA. A liberation of "Charlie's Point."
California Dreaming, American International, USA. A born again beach blanket flick.
Ocean Motion, Mike Moir, USA.

1980
Balinese Surfer, Bill Leimbach, USA. A study of Balinese boys integrating surfing into their traditional lifestyle.
Fall Line, Nat Young, Australia. Study of how both skiers and surfers look for the line across a wave or down a mountain which will give the greatest speed.
Fantasea, Greg Huglin, USA. Many rich sequences of very different surfers: Mark Richards, Chris Byrne, Bobby Owens, Mark Foo.
Seaflight, Bob and Ron Condon, USA.

1981
Bali High, Stephen Spaulding and Alexis Thomas, Indonesia. With Peter McCabe at Padang Padang.
Crystal Eyes, Yuri Farrant, USA. Beautifully edited footage of Hawaii — good windsurfing.
Pacific Dreams, Chris Bystrom, USA. Joe Roper ripping Big Rock in San Diego and Buttons at Velzyland.

THE SURF MOVIE

Tales of the Seven Seas, Scott Dittrich, USA. Good surf from around the world, including Bali, Brazil and Oregon(?). Five cameramen on three continents.
Thunder Down Under, Chris Bystrom, USA. Lots of uncrowded point surf in the Southern Hemisphere.
We Got Surf, Hal Jepson, USA. Footage of Simon Anderson testing a new Thruster in Mexico; Shaun Tomson carving Swamis.

1982
Adventures in Paradise, Scott Dittrich, USA. Beautiful Maalaea and some of the first films of Nias.
Fast Times at Ridgemont High, Universal Motion Pictures, USA. Based on the book by Cameron Crowe. Starring Sean Penn as the San Diego surfer-doper Jeff Spicoli.
Band on the Run, Harry Hodge, Australia. A long delayed film about a group of Australian surfers looking for the perfect wave.
Storm Riders, David Lourie, Jack McCoy, Dick Hoole, Australia. One of the most publicized films ever. Lopez flowing at Grajagan, and Wayne Bartholomew riding Burleigh with his head grooving the roof of the barrel are highlights.
Surf Attack, Jack and Clark Poling, USA. East Coast surfers ripping.

1983
Blazing Boards, Chris Bystrom, USA. Action from 1982 and 1983, featuring Tom Carrol, Tom Curren, Martin Potter and Marvin Foster.
Follow the Sun, Scott Dittrich, USA. Featuring exotic locales, Tom Curren at Hawaii's North Shore, slow-motion photography of Shaun Tomson, and Dane Kealoha.
Free Ride Final Edition, Bill Delaney, USA. Some new footage of the 1982 pro season, along with the best of the original film. Michael Ho's surfing during the Pipe Masters is stunning.
Full Blast, Curt Mastalka, USA. A close look at Hawaii's young hot doggers.
Kong's Island, David Lourie, Dick Hoole, Jack McCoy, Australia. A documentary profiling Gary "Kong" Elkerton and his friends Rabbit Bartholomew and Chappy Jennings.
Ocean Fever, Steve Soderberg, USA.
Puberty Blues, Bruce Beresford, Australia. A satire of Sydney-area surfers, based on a novel by two former surfer groupies.
Sea Flight II, A Condon Production, USA. Re-release of **Sea Flight** with new footage of Marvin Foster, Buttons Kaluhiokalani, Bertlemann, Michael and Derek Ho at Ala Mo.
Storm Riders, Dick Hoole, Jack McCoy, David Lourie, USA. Edited version of the original film with the short "Kong's Island."

BIBLIOGRAPHY

Poised like otherworldly astronauts in a cloud-like medium are three more Makapuu body surfers by Levin.

Anonymous. "A Day With Duke Kahanamoku." *Paradise of the Pacific* 62 (12):16–17, December 1950.

———. "Duke Kahanamoku . . . Mr. Ambassador." *Paradise of the Pacific* 72 (5):10–11, May 1960.

———. "Hawaii's Duke." *Paradise of the Pacific* 73 (7):September 1961.

———. "Let's Go Surfing." *Paradise of the Pacific* 70 (3):9–11, March 1958.

———. "Surf Boarding." *Lahaina Historical Guide.* Honolulu: Star Bulletin Print Co.:2–3. 1961.

———. "Surfing at Waikiki." *Paradise of the Pacific* 66:24–25, 119, Annual 1954.

———. "Surfboarding in 1855, at Kealakekua, Hawaii." *Knickerbocker Magazine,* August, 1855.

———. "Surf Riding — He'e Nalu." *Paradise of the Pacific* 49 (10):21–22, October 1937.

———. "Surf Riding Photographer Clarence Maki." *Paradise of the Pacific* 67 (6):12–13, June 1955.

———. "The Wave." *San Francisco Magazine,* December 17, 1898.

———. "Two great surfing dates in January: 15, 22. Then the champs of the world vie for honors in the big surf at Makaha." *Paradise of the Pacific* 68 (1):9–11, January 1956.

———. "Waikiki Surf Club." *Paradise of the Pacific* 60 (9):6–8, September 1948.

Allen, Jim. *Locked In: Surfing for Life.* Cranbury, N.J.: Barnes. 1970.

Andrews, Lorrin. *A Dictionary of the Hawaiian Language.* Honolulu: Henry M. Whitney. 1865.

Ball, John Heath ("Doc"). *California Surfriders.* Los Angeles: Mountain & Sea Books. 1979.

Bascom, Willard. *Waves and Beaches*. New York: Doubleday & Co., Inc. 1964.

Bates, George W. (A haole). *Sandwich Island Notes*. London: Simpson, Low, Son and Co. 1854.

Beaglehole, Ernest. "Culture Peaks in Polynesia." *Man* 37:138–140. 1937.

Beckwith, Martha W. "The Hawaiian Romance of Laieikawai." *Bureau of American Ethnology, Thirty-third Annual World Report*: 285–666. 1919.

_____. *Hawaiian Mythology*. New Haven: Yale University Press. 1940.

Best, Elsdon. *Games and Pastimes of the Maori*. Wellington: Dominion Museum Bulletin 8:1926.

Bingham, Hiram. *A Residence of Twenty-one Years in the Sandwich Islands*. New York: Sherman Converse. 1847.

Bird, Isabella Lucy. *The Hawaiian Archipelago — Six Months Among the Palm Groves, Coral Reefs, and Volcanoes of the Sandwich Islands*. London: 1875.

Black, Kerry P. *Wave transformation over shallow reef: Field Measurements and Data Analysis*. Honolulu: Look Laboratory of Oceanographic Engineering 42:1978.

Blake, Thomas Edward. *Hawaiian Surfboard*. Honolulu: Paradise of the Pacific Press. 1935.

_____. *Hawaiian Surfriding: The Ancient and Royal Pastime*. Flagstaff, Arizona: Northland Press. 1961.

_____. "Surfboard Technique." *Paradise of the Pacific* 47 (2):17–22, February 1935.

Bloomfield, John. *Know-How in the Surf*. Rutland, Vt.: Tuttle, 1965.

Boddam-Whetham, J. W. *Pearls of the Pacific*. London: Hurst and Blockett. 1876.

Bowen, Robert S. *Wipeout*. New York: Criterion Books. 1969.

Brennan, Joseph. *Duke of Hawaii*.

New York: Ballantine Books. 1968.

_____. *Duke Kahanamoku, Hawaii's Golden Man*. Honolulu: Hogarth Press. 1974.

Buck, Peter H. *Arts and Crafts of Hawaii*. Honolulu: Bishop Museum, Special Publication 45. 1957.

Calisch, Ruston M. *Paumalu*. San Clemente: Paumalu Press. 1979.

Carter, Jeff. *Surf Beaches of Australia's East Coast*. Sydney: Angus & Robertson. 1968.

Caton, John D. *Miscellanies*. Boston: Houghton, Osgood and Co. 1880.

Cheever, H. T. *Life in the Sandwich Islands*. New York: Barnes. 1851.

Clark, John R. K. *The Beaches of Oahu*. Honolulu: University Press of Hawaii. 1977.

_____. *The Beaches of Maui County*. Honolulu: University Press of Hawaii. 1980.

Cleary, William. *Surfing: All the Young Wave Hunters*. New York: The New American Library, Inc. 1967.

Clemens, Samuel (pseud., Mark Twain). "Surf-Bathing in the Sandwich Islands." *Sacramento Union*. 1866.

Cook, James. *A Voyage to the Pacific Ocean . . . for Making Discoveries in the Northern Hemisphere in . . . the 'Resolution' and 'Discovery.'"* London: Nicol and Cadell. 1784. 3 vols. and atlas (vol. 3 by James King).

_____. *A Voyage to the Pacific Ocean, Undertaken by the Command of His Majesty, for Making Discoveries in the Northern Hemisphere*. London: Hakluyt Society. 1785.

Cook, Joseph J., and Romeika, William J. *Better Surfing for Boys*. New York: Dodd, Mead. 1967.

Corps of Engineers Technical Report No. 4, Beach Erosion Board. *Shore*

Protection Planning and Design. Washington, D.C.: U.S. Government Printing Office. 1961.

Crowe, Cameron. *Fast Times at Ridgemont High*. New York: Simon and Schuster. 1981.

Daws, Gavan. *Shoal of Time: A History of the Hawaiian Islands*. New York: Macmillan. 1968.

Defant, Albert. *Ebb and Flow*. Ann Arbor: University of Michigan Press. 1958.

Dept. of Land and Natural Resources, Hawaii. *Report to the Sixth Legislature of the State of Hawaii on Senate Resolution no. 290, Regular Session on 1971, Sixth Legislature of the State of Hawaii: relating to surfing sites*. 1971.

Dewey, Nelson. *How to Body Surf*. Canada: Saltaire Publishing Co., 1970.

Dibble, Sheldon. *A History of the Sandwich Islands*. Honolulu: T. G. Thrum. 1909.

Dixon, Peter L. *The Complete Book of Surfing*. New York: Coward, McCann & Geoghegan. 1967.

_____. *Where the Surfers Are: A Guide to the World's Great Surfing Spots*. New York: Coward, McCann & Geoghegan. 1968.

_____. *Men Who Ride Mountains*. New York: Bantam Books. 1969.

Douglas, Diana. *Surfing Nurse*. Sydney, Australia: Horwitz Publications. 1971.

Drummond, Ron. *The Art of Wave Riding*. Hollywood: Cloister Press. 1931.

Edwards, Phil. *You Should Have Been Here an Hour Ago: The Stoked Side of Surfing*. New York: Harper & Row. 1967.

Ellis, William. *Polynesian Researches.* 4 vols. London: Fisher and Jackson. 1831.

Emerson, Nathaniel B. "Causes of the Decline of Ancient Hawaiian Sports." *The Friend* (Honolulu) 50:57–60, 1892.

———. *Unwritten Literature of Hawaii.* Washington: Bureau of American Ethnology, Bulletin 38. 1909.

Emory, Kenneth P. "Sports, Games and Amusements." *Ancient Hawaiian Civilization.* Honolulu: Kamehameha Schools, 1933, chapter 14.

———. *Origin of the Hawaiians.* Honolulu: B. P. Bishop Museum, 1911.

Farrelly, Midget and McGregor, Craig. *This Surfing Life.* Adelaide, Australia: Rigby Ltd. 1965.

Filosa, Gary Fairmont, II. *The Surfer's Almanac: An International Surfing Guide.* Canada: Clarke, Irwin & Co. 1977.

———. *Surfing: How, When, Where.* Fountain Valle, Ca.: Coastline Community College. 1977.

Finney, Ben R. "Surfboarding in Oceania: its Pre-European Distribution." *Wiener Völkerkundliche Mitteilungen.* 1959.

———. *Hawaiian Surfing, a Study of Cultural Change.* Unpublished M.A. thesis, no. 405, University of Hawaii. 1959.

———. "The Development and Diffusion of Modern Hawaiian Surfing." *The Journal of the Polynesian Society* 69 (4):315–331, December 1960.

———. "The Surfing Community: Contrasting values between the local and California surfers in Hawaii." *Social Progress* (Honolulu) 23:73–76, 1959.

Finney, Ben, and Houston, James D. *Surfing: The Sport of Hawaiian Kings.* Rutland, Vt.: Tuttle. 1966.

Ford, Alexander H. "Out-Door Allurements." in Thrum's *Hawaiian Annual,* Honolulu: Honolulu Star Bulletin Print Co. 149–149. 1911.

Fornander, Abraham. *An Account of the Polynesian Race, its Origin and Migrations.* 3 vols. London: Trubner and Co. 1878–1885.

———. *An Account of the Polynesian Race, its Origin and Migrations and the Ancient History of the Hawaiian People to the Times of King Kamehameha I.* Rutland, Vt.: Tuttle. 1969. First published in 1880.

———. *Fornander Collection of Hawaiian Antiquities and Folklore.* 3 vols. Honolulu: Bishop Museum, Memoir vols. 4, 5, 6. 1916–1920.

Gardner, Robert. *The Art of Body Surfing.* Philadelphia: Chilton. 1972.

Gassner, Julius S. *Voyages and Adventures of La Pérouse.* Honolulu: University of Hawaii Press. 1969.

Gerritson, Franciscus. *Beach and Surf Parameters in Hawaii.* Honolulu: University of Hawaii Sea Grant College Program. 1978.

Giles, Michael L. *Wave and current conditions for various modifications of Kewalo Basin, Honolulu, Oahu, Hawaii: Hydraulic Model Investigation: Final Report.* Vicksburg: U.S. Army Engineer Waterways Experiment Station. H-75-15.

Gosline, W. A. and Brock, Vernon. *Handbook of Hawaiian Fishes.* Honolulu: University of Hawaii Press. 1970.

Grigg, Richard W. and Church, Ron. *Surfer in Hawaii: A Guide to Surfing in the Hawaiian Islands.* Dana Point, Ca.: John Severson Publications. 1963.

Grissim, John. *Pure Stoke.* New York: Harper & Row, Publishers, Inc. 1982.

Gurrey, A. R. *The Surf Riders of Hawaii.* Honolulu: A. H. Gurrey. 1914.

Hale, Louis "Sally". "Waikiki's Wild Waves." *Forecast:* 6, July 1951.

Hemmings, Fred. *Surfing: Hawaii's Gift to the World of Sports.* Tokyo: Zokeisha Publications. 1977.

Hill, S. S. "Native Men, Women and Children in Surf at Kailua, Hawaii." *Travels:* 196–202. 1849.

Holmes, Paul. *Surfabout.* Darlinghurst, NSW: Soundtracks Publishing Co. Pty. Ltd. 1980.

———. *World of Surfing.* New York: Grosset & Dunlap. 1968.

Houston, James D. *A Native Son of the Golden West.* New York: Ballantine Books, Inc. 1972.

I'i, John Papa. *Fragments of Hawaiian History,* trans. Mary Kawena Pukui, ed. Dorothey B. Barrer. Honolulu: Bishop Museum Press. 1959.

Jarves, James J. *History of the Hawaiian or Sandwich Islands.* London: Edward Moxon. 1843.

———. *Scenes and Scenery in the Sandwich Islands.* London: 1844.

Kahanamoku, Duke P. "Riding the Surfboard." *Mid-Pacific Magazine:* 3–10, January 1911.

———. "Riding the Surfboard." *Mid-Pacific Magazine:* 151–158, February 1911.

Kahanamoku, Duke with Brennan, Joe. *World of Surfing.* New York: Grosset & Dunlap. 1968.

Kahn, David. "Mountaineers of the Sea." *Paradise of the Pacific* 74 (10):47–50, November 1962.

Kalakaua, David. *The Legends and Myths of Hawaii.* New York: C. L. Webster & Co. 1888.

Keauokalani, Kepelino. *Traditions of Hawaii.* Honolulu: B. P. Bishop Museum. 1932.

Kelly, John M. *Surf & Sea.* Cranbury, N.J.: Barnes. 1965.

_____. *Surf Parameters; Part II, Social and Historical Dimensions.* Honolulu: Look Laboratory of Oceanographic Engineering. University of Hawaii. 1973.

King, C. A. M. *Beaches and Coasts.* New York: St. Martin's Press. 1960.

Kinghorn, Kenneth B. *One Ride, One Life.* Unpublished Ph.D. thesis, no. 891, University of Hawaii. 1976.

Kinstle, James. *Surfboard Design and Construction.* Manhattan Beach, Ca.: Natural High Express Publishing Company. 1975.

Kirk, Cameron and Hanle, Zack. *The Surfer's Handbook.* New York: Dell Publishing Co., Inc. 1968.

Klein, H. Arthur. *Surfing.* Philadelphia: Lippincott. 1965.

_____. *Surf-Riding.* Philadelphia: Lippincott. 1972.

Klein, H. Arthur, and Klein, M. C. *Surf's Up! An Anthology of Surfing.* Indianapolis: Bobbs-Merrill. 1966.

Kuhns, Grant W. *On Surfing.* Rutland, Vt.: Tuttle. 1963.

Kuykendall, Ralph S. *The Hawaiian Kingdom, 1778–1854: Foundation and Transformation.* Honolulu: University of Hawaii Press. 1947.

_____. *The Hawaiian Kingdom, 1854–1974: Twenty Critical Years.* Honolulu: University of Hawaii Press, 1953.

_____. *The Hawaiian Kingdom, 1874–1893: The Kalakaua Dynasty.* Honolulu: University of Hawaii Press, 1967.

LeBlond, Paul H. and Mysak, Lawrence A. *Waves in the Ocean.* Amsterdam, N.Y.: Elsevier Scientific Publishing Co. 1978.

Lee, T. T., et. al. *Wave action in Haleiwa Harbor, Hawaii: Hydraulic Model Investigation.* Honolulu: Look Laboratory of Oceanographic Engineering. Technical report no. 32.

_____. *Wave attenuation and wave-induced setup over shallow reefs: Narrative project as of 30 April 1977.* Honolulu: Look Laboratory of Oceanographic Engineering, Report no. 15.

Lind, Andrew. *Hawaii's People.* Honolulu: University of Hawaii Press. 1955.

London, Jack. *On the Makaloa Mat.* New York: Macmillan Co. 1920.

_____. *The Cruise of the Snark.* New York: Macmillan Co. 1977.

_____. "The Psychology of the Surfboard." *Mid-Pacific Magazine:* 437–441, May 1915.

Lorch, Carlos. *Lopez, The Classic Hawaiian Surfer.* Redondo Beach, Ca.: Mountain and Sea. 1982.

Macfarlane, Walter. "More and Better Sports for Waikiki." *Paradise of the Pacific* 51(10):5–6, October 1939.

MacKellar, Jean Scott. "Surfriding." *Paradise of the Pacific* 72(10): 59–61, 108, November 1960.

Madison, Arnold. *Surfing, Basic Techniques.* New York: McKay. 1979.

Malo, David. *Hawaiian Antiquities.* 2d ed. Bishop Museum, Special Publication 2. Honolulu: Hawaiian Gazette Co. 1951.

Margan, Frank, and Finney, Ben R. *A Pictorial History of Surfing.* London: Hamlyn. 1970.

Mason, George William. *Practical surf forecasting by means of spectral analysis of sea surface elevation.* Unpublished M.S. thesis, no. 1518, University of Hawaii. 1977.

Matwell, C. Bede. *Surf: Australians Against the Sea.* Sydney: Angus and Robertson. 1949.

Mayo, Donald Sherwood. "How to make your own . . . Surfboard." *Paradise of the Pacific* 66(8):24, 28, August 1954.

_____. "Island Profile: Royal Hawaiian Champ of the Champs . . . Duke Kahanamoku." *Paradise of the Pacific* 68(6):127, June 1956.

McClelland, Gordon. *Rick Griffin.* New York: Perigee Books. 1980.

McGregor, Craig. *This Surfing Life.* Adelaide: Rigby. 1965.

Minikin, R.C.R. *Winds, Waves and Maritime Structures.* London: Charles Griffin and Company. 1950.

Minvielle, A. E. "Canoe Surfing by 'Toots.'" *Forecast* 12(12):13, 40, 1953.

Morgan, Patrick. *Scarlet Surf at Makaha.* New York: Macfadden-Bartell Corp. 1970.

Muirhead, Desmond. *Surfing in Hawaii: A Personal Memoir.* Flagstaff, Ariz.: Northland Press. 1962.

Munk, Walter H. *Wave Action on Structures.* New York: American Institute of Mining and Metallurgical Engineers, no. 2322. 1948.

Nelson, William Desmond. *Surfing: A Handbook.* Philadelphia: Auerbach. 1973.

Nordhoff, Charles. *Northern California, Oregon, and the Sandwich Islands.* New York: Harper & Bros. 1874.

Olney, Ross R. *The Young Sportsman's Guide to Surfing.* Canada: Scholastic Book Services. 1968.

Olney, Ross R. and Graham, Richard W., *The Kings of the Surf.* New York: G.P. Putnam's Sons. 1969.

Patterson, Otto B. *Surf-Riding: Its Thrills and Techniques.* Rutland, Vt.: Tuttle. 1960.

Pearson, Kent. *Surfing Subcultures of Australia and New Zealand.* Australia: University of Queensland Press. 1979.

Phinzy, Coles. "New Songs of Old Hawaii." *Sports Illustrated:* 38–51, November 10, 1958.

Pierce, Richard A. *Russia's Hawaiian Adventure, 1815–1817.* Berkeley: University of California Press. 1965.

Pitchford, Genie. "Surfboarding in Hawaii." *Paradise of the Pacific* 52(1):27–28, January 1940.

Poepoe, Sam. "Surfing at Waikiki." *Forecast* 9(12):4–5, 29, 1950.

⸺. "Surfing at Waikiki." *Forecast* 12(12):202–22, 1953.

Pollard, Jack. *The Australian Surfrider.* Sydney: Murray. 1963.

⸺. *The Surfrider.* New York: Taplinger. 1968.

Prytherch, Reginald John. *Surfing: A Modern Guide.* London: Faber & Faber. 1972.

Pukui, Mary K. "Songs (meles) of Old Ka'u, Hawaii," *Journal of American Folklore* 62:247–258. 1949.

Pukui, Mary K., and Elbert, Samuel H. *Hawaiian-English Dictionary.* Honolulu: University of Hawaii Press. 1957.

Pukui, Mary Kawena; Elbert, Samuel H.; and Mookini, Esther T. *Place Names of Hawaii.* Honolulu: University of Hawaii Press. 1974.

Russell, R.C.H., and Macmillan, D.H. *Waves and Tides.* New York: Philosophical Library. 1953.

St. Pierre, Brian. *The Fantastic Plastic Voyage: Across the South Pacific with Surfers and a Camera.* New York: Coward, McCann & Geoghegan. 1969.

Severson, John Hugh. *Great Surfing: Photos, Stories, Essays, Reminiscences, and Poems.* Garden City, N.Y.: Doubleday. 1967.

⸺. *Modern Surfing Around the World.* Garden City, N.Y.: Doubleday. 1964.

Shaw, Stephen M. *The Surfboard Builder's Manual.* La Mesa, Ca.: Products Unlimited, 1969.

⸺. *Surfboard.* La Mesa, Ca.: Transmedia. 1983.

Shepard, F.P. *Submarine Geology.* New York: Harper and Brothers. 1948.

Silverman, Arthur L. "Surf, Sun and Summer School on Hawaii's Far Famed 'Rainbow' Campus." *Paradise of the Pacific* 68:8–9, Annual 1956.

Simpson, Flora Lee. "The Sport of Hawaiian Kings." *Paradise of the Pacific* 56(2):22, February 1944.

Smith, Gene. "Surfboarding from Molokai to Oahu." *Paradise of the Pacific* 52(8):21–24, August 1940.

Smith, S. Peroy. "Use of the surfboard in New Zealand." *Journal of the Polynesian Society* 30:50, 1921.

Spinner, Stephanie. *Water Skiing and Surfboarding.* New York: Golden Press. 1968.

Stern, David H., and Cleary, William S. *Surfing Guide to Southern California.* Malibu, Ca.: Fitzpatrick. 1963.

Stewart, C.S. *A Residence in the Sandwich Islands.* Boston: Weeks, Jordan and Co. 1839.

⸺. "Surfing in Lahaina in 1824." *Stewart's Sandwich Islands.* 5th ed. 196–7.

Stokes, J.F.G. "Heiaus of Hawaii." Honolulu: Bishop Museum, ms. 1919.

Sutrin, Mark. *Surfing: How to Improve Your Technique.* New York: Watts. 1973.

Taylor, Clarice B. "Tales about Hawaii." *Honolulu Star-Bulletin* November 26:20. 1958.

The American National Red Cross. *Swimming and Water Safety.* 1973.

The Surfboard Builders' Yearbook. La Mesa, Ca.: Transmedia. 1971.

Thomson, Carl. *Surfing in Great Britain.* London: Constable. 1972.

Thrum, Thomas G. *Hawaiian Folktales.* Chicago: McClurg. 1907.

⸺. "Hawaiian Surf Riding." *Hawaiian Almanac and Annual for 1896:* 106–113. Trans. from a Hawaiian manuscript.

⸺. "Kelea, the Surf Rider." *Hawaiian Almanac and Annual* 57:58–62. 1931.

⸺. "Surf Bathing." *The Hawaiian Almanac and Annual* 8:52, 1882.

⸺. "Waikiki Surf Riding." *Hawaiian Almanac and Annual* 34:112, 1908.

⸺. *The Hawaiian Almanac and Annual for 1910.* Honolulu: Thomas G. Thrum. 1910.

Thurston, Lorrin P. "Surf-Board Riding in Hawaii." *The Mid-Pacific Magazine* 9(4):317–325, 1915.

Todaro, Anthony. "Waikiki's Famous Beach Beach Boys." *Paradise of the Pacific* 64:104–106, 124, Annual 1953.

Tregaskis, Richard W. "Man in Search of a Perfect Beach." *Paradise of the Pacific* 74(1):16–11, January 1962.

⸺. *Quest continued Paradise of the Pacific* 74(8):19–24, September 1962.

Turnball, John. *A Voyage Round the World in the Years 1800, 1801, 1802, 1803, and 1804.* 2d ed. London: A. Maxwell. 1813.

Turner, George. *Nineteen Years in Polynesia: Missionary Life, Travels, and Researches in the Islands of the Pacific.* London: J. Snow, 1861.

Twain, Mark. *Mark Twain's Letters from Hawaii.* New York: Appleton-Century. 1966.

———. *Roughing It.* Hartford, Ct.: American Publishing Co. 1872.

University of Hawaii, Department of Geography. *Atlas of Hawaii.* Honolulu: University of Hawaii Press, 1973.

University of Hawaii Sea Grant Marine Advisory Program. *Bodysurfing Safety.* Honolulu: 1976.

Vallis, George. "The Drama of Surfing." *Paradise of the Pacific* 62(12):24–25, December 1950.

Wagenvoord, James, and Bailey, Lynn. *How to Surf.* New York: Macmillan. 1968.

Waimau, J., "Ancient Sports of Hawaii." *Kuokoa* (newspaper) trans. Mary K. Pukui, Honolulu, December 23, 1865.

Walker, James R. *Recreational Surf Parameters.* Honolulu: Look Laboratory of Oceanographic Engineering, University of Hawaii. 1974.

———. *Surfing assessment: Ala Wai Small Boat Harbor, Oahu, Hawaii.* Honolulu: Look Laboratory of Oceanographic Engineering. Report no. 7.

———. *Wave transformation over a sloping bottom and over a three-dimensional shoal.* Unpublished Ph.D. thesis, University of Hawaii, 1974.

Warwick, Wayne. *Surfriding in New Zealand.* Wellington: Seven Seas. 1968.

Wenkam, Robert. *Hawaii: Kauai, Oahu, Maui, Molokai, Hawaii and Lanai.* Rand McNally. 1972.

Westervelt, W. D. *Legends of Maui, a Demigod of Polynesia and of His Mother Hina.* Melbourne: George Robertson. 1960.

———. *Legends of Old Hawaii.* Boston: Ellis Press. 1915.

———. "Story of the Hawaiian Board." *The Friend:* 83–84, April 1916.

Wilson, Gary. *Surfing in Hawaii.* Honolulu: World Wide Distributor.

Wolfe, Tom. *The Pump House Gang.* New York: Farrar, Straus and Giroux. 1968.

Wright, Bank. *Surfing California.* Redondo Beach, Ca.: Manana. 1973.

———. *Surfing Hawaii.* Redondo Beach, Ca.: Mountain & Sea. 1971.

Young, Nat. *Nat Young's Book of Surfing: The Fundamentals and Adventures of Board-Riding.* Sydney: Reed. 1979.

———. *The History of Surfing.* Sydney: Palm Beach Press. 1983.

Zahn, Thomas C. "Surfboarding from Molokai to Waikiki." *Paradise of the Pacific* 66(3):26–28, 32, March 1954.

SURFING PERIODICALS

Monthlies:

Action Now. Surfer Publishing Group, Inc: P.O. Box 1028, Dana Point, CA 92629.

Backdoor. Progress Press, Moorabbin: Australia.

Pacific Lines. Lozano Enterprises: 1001 W. 17th St., Suite R, Costa Mesa, CA 92627.

Surfer. Box 1028, Dana Point, CA 92629.

Surfing. Western Empire Publications: 2720 Camino Capistrano, Box 3010, San Clemente, CA 92672.

Surfin' Life. Marine Planning Co., Ltd.: NS Bldg. 2-2-3, Sarugaku-Cho, Chiyoda-Ku, Tokyo, Japan.

Surfing Classic. Surfing Classic Magazine; Ito Building, 4-4 Hongoku-Cho, Nihonbashi, Chuo-Ku, Tokyo, Japan.

Surfing World. Surfing World Magazine: P.O. Box 128, Mona Vale, NSW 2103, Australia.

The Surf Report. A Surfer Publication: P.O. Box 1029, Dana Point, CA 92629.

Tracks. Soundtracts Publishing Pty. Ltd.: P.O. Box 746, Darlinghurst, NSW 2010, Australia.

Bi-monthlies:

Breakout. A California Corporation: Post Office Box 820, Carlsbad, CA 92008.

Hawaii Surf & Sea. Hawaii Surf & Sea, Inc.: 1387 Queen Emma St., Honolulu, Hawaii 96813.

Sea Notes. John Witzig and Company Pty. Ltd.: P.O. Box 34, Avalon Beach, N.S.W. 2107, Australia.

Surfing Classic. Tokyo: Ito Building, 4-4 Hongoku-Cho, Nihonbashi, Chuo-Ku, Tokyo, Japan.

U.S. Surf. Coastline Productions, Inc. 320 N. Atlantic Ave., Cocoa Beach, Florida 32931.

Waves. Murray Publishers Pty. Ltd.: 154 Clarence St., Sydney 2000, Australia.

Quarterlies:

Zig Zag. South African Promotions: P.O. Box 10685, Marine Parade, 4056, Durban, South Africa.

Note: Some of the above periodicals may have ceased publication as of press time.

INDEX

A

Ab (San Diego area, Calif.), 134

An Account of the Polynesian Race: Its Origins and Migrations (journal article), 30, 33

"Ace Cool." *See* Cooke, Alec.

Ahuea, Premier, 51

Aikau, Eddie, 197
comments about racist treatment of himself in South Africa, 198

Ala Moana Beach (Honolulu), 9

alaia (type of surfboard), 41

Alakea Slip (Honolulu Harbor), 88

Allen, R. Paul, 147, 149

Allied Surf Association of the South China Sea, 195

Almond, Elliott
comments about surfing in Orange County, Calif., 133

Alter, Hobie, 114, 118– 119, 133

Amalu, Charles, 78

Amateur Athletic Union (AAU), 88

American International Pictures (AIP), 124, 127, 128

American Latex Company, 114

The American Red Cross
Duke Kahanamoku and, 96

"Ancient Workshop of the Hawaii Islanders" (archaeological study), 33

Apocalypse Now (movie), 138
still from the movie, 138– 139

Arago, Jacques, 35

Association of Surfing Professionals (ASP), 165

The Astronauts, 136

Atlantic City, 92

August, Robert, 146, 147, 188

Australia
Duke Kahanamoku in, 92, 94, 94, 95
surfers from, 153, 154
surfing in, 92, 95, 114, 150, 153
surfing meets, 162, 165

Australian Crawl, 91

Australian Professional Surfing Association, 165

Australian Swimming Association, 92

Avalon, Frankie, 124, 127, 134

The Azores, 188

B

Bailey, Jim, *112*

Balboa (Calif.), *83*, 104

Bali, 165, 188, 191, *192*, 195

Ball, John Heath "Doc,"
comments about George Freeth rescue missions in Calif., 104

Ballentyne, Watson, 74

balsa (in surfboards), 111, 113

Banzai Pipeline (Hawaii), 11, 162, 170– 171, 172– 173, 176

Baptiste, Panama, 78, 79

Bart, Peter
comments about beach blanket movies, 128

Bartholomew, Wayne "Rabbit," 154

Bartlett, Charles William
ukiyo-e style surfing print by, *58– 59*

Bay of Plenty (South Africa), *194– 195*

Beach Ball (movie), 128

Beach Blanket Bingo (movie), 127

The Beach Boys, 134, 136

The Beach Girls and the Monster (movie), 124

Beach Party (movie), 124, 127, 128

beachboys
California, 133
Waikiki, 74, 77– 78, 79, 96

Beamer, Winona
comments about learning hula by watching the surf, 33– 34

The Beatles, 137

Beckley, Mrs. George, 74

Begg, S.
surfing engraving by, *69*

Bell's Beach Classic, 162

Berry, Chuck, 134

Berry, Jan. 130

Bertlemann, Larry, *13*

Bikini Beach (movie), 127

Bingham, Rev. Hiram
comments about
the barbaric appearance of the Hawaiians, 54
first seeing naked surfers and swimmers upon his arrival, 38
The decline of surfing, 54

Bishop, Isabella L. Bird

comments about
surfboards being used in Hilo in the 1870s, 52
surfing, 52

Blake, Tom, 34, 80, 81– 82
comments about
Duke's surfing demonstrations on the mainland, 96
meeting Duke Kahanamoku, 81
inventing the first hollow surfboard, 81– 82
decal, *106*
George Freeth and, 107
invents the skeg, 107, 109
the "Hawaiian Hollow Surfboard" and, 107
windsurfing and, 200

"Blake's cigar," 82

Blazing Boards (movie)
poster from, *141*

Blonde (ship), 42

Bluff Cove (Calif.), 109

boardsailing, 11, 200

"Boneyard" (Doheny Beach, Calif.), 8

Boomerang Club (Sydney), *94*

Bowman, Pierre, 198

Boyd, Duke
comments about surfing, 10

Bradshaw, Ken, *21*

Brazil, 165

Brown, Bruce, 133, 137, 144, 146, 147, 149
comments about following summer swells, 147

Brown, Woody, 117

Browne, Bud, 150

Buckley, Brian, *170– 171*

Budi, I Made
Balinese painting by, *189*

Burrhead, 117

Byrnes, Edd "Kookie," 128, 134

Byron, Capt. George Anson
comments about the maintenance of surfboards in 1825, 42

C

Cabell, Joey, 99, 153

Cadiz (Spain), 188

Cairns, Ian, 165

California
Duke in, 92, 96, 97, 100
surf cult, 124, 127, 128, 130, 133, 134, 136, 137
surfing in, 8, 9, 70, 73, 104– 105, 107, 109, 111, 113– 114

See also specific beach names.

California Surfriders (book), 104

Campbell, Archibald
comments about Hawaiians as good swimmers, 50

Campbell, John, 191

canoe leaping, 43, 46

canoes, 44– 45, 47, 74, 78

Carillo Beach (Calif.), 128

Carroll, Tom, *19*

Castle's Point (Hawaii), 73

Center, George D. "Dad", 73, 81, 96

Chambre d'Amour (France), 188

Chandler, Norman B.
comments about California beachboys-turned-successful-businessmen, 133

Chandler, Otis
comments about surfing, 9– 10

The Chantays, 134

chants, 33– 34
"surf coaxing rituals" – , 30, 33
wave-generating wind – , 33

Chapman, Ray, *199*

Charlot, John
comments about chanting, 33

Cheever, Rev. Henry T.
comments about surfing, 50, 51

Christian, Roger, 130

Clark, Gordon "Grubby," 114, 119, 133

Clarke, Waltah, 79

Cleary, Bill,
comments about surfing abroad
in Cadiz, 188
in Cornwall, 188– 191

Coca-Cola bottling company (Sydney), 162, 165

Columbia Pictures, 130

Compson, Betty, 64

Cooke, Capt. James, 34, 49, 54
comments about
canoe leaping, 46
surfing, 10– 11
engraving of the arrival of – at Kealakekua, *44– 45*

Cooke, Alec, *14– 15*

Cornwall (England), 191

Corona Del Mar (Calif.) 82, 92

Corona Del Mar Surf Board

Club, 107

Cottrell, W. A. (Knute), 74, 75

Crabbe, Buster, 98

Crane, Ted, 117

Crawford, Jeff, *150– 151*

Cronulla Beach (Australia), 165

The Cruise of the Snark (book), 68

Curren, Tommy, 154, *163*, 165

Curtis, Tony, 127

D

"Dad." *See* Center, George D.

Dahlin, Dale, *182*

Dana Point (Calif.), 119, 133, 134

Daniels, Charles M., 88, 91

Daniels, Chick, 78, 79

Darren, James, 124

d'Auezac, Gerard, *190– 191*

Davey, Frank, 54

"Death of a Gremmie" (song), 136

"Decals in Excess" (painting), *120– 121*

Dee, Sandra, 124

Dick Dale and the Del Tones, 128, 134, 136

Discovery (ship), 49

diseases
effects of – on surfing, 54

Doheny Beach (Calif.), 8, 134

Dole, Sanford B., 74

Don't Make Waves (movie), 127

"Don't Make Waves" (song), 127

Dora, Mickey "Da Cat," 124, *128– 129*

Downing, George, 117

Doyle, Mike, 153, 162

"Dudie." *See* Miller, Edward Kenneth Kaleleihealani.

Duke. *See* Kahanamoku, Duke.

Duke Kahanamoku Invitational Surfing Championships, 98, 162
See also Duke Kahanamoku Hawaiian Surfing Classic.

Duke Kahanamoku Hawaiian Surfing Classic (formerly known as the Duke Kahanamoku Invitational Surfing Championships), 162

Durban 500 surfing meet, 198

E

Eddy, Duane, 134
education
  effects of Western — on surfing, 54
Edwards, Phil, 133
El Monte Legion Stadium (Calif.), 134
Ellis, William
  comments about Hawaiians' fondness for swimming and surfing, 50
  maintenance of the surfboard in 1822, 41
  surfing among the kings, 38
Emerson, Nathaniel B.
  comments about the decline of surfing, 54
The Endless Summer (movie), 137, 144, 146, 147, 149, 188
  poster, *137*
Evans, Jim
  paintings by, *120–121, 147*

F

Fabares, Shelley, 130
Fain, Johnny, 124, *131*
Fairy Bower (Manly Beach, Australia), 165
Farrelly, Bernard "Midget," 153
Fast Times at Ridgemont High (novel and movie), 9
Feldman, Paul
  comments about Brian Wilson, 136
Ferriman, Stewart, 169
Fine (magazine), 197
Finney, Ben
  comments about surfing in Oceania, 34, 37
fins, fiberglass, 113
Fisher, Jim, 117
Five Summer Stories (movie), 140
Fletcher, Herbie, *155*
Ford, Alexander Hume, 68, 70, 73, 74
  comments about the Outrigger Club, 68, 70
Fornander, Abraham, 30
Forte, Fabian, 130
France, 133, 165, 188, 195
Freeth, George, 68, 70, 73, 77, 92
  bust of, *104, 105, 105*
Freshwater (Australia), 95
Froiseth, Wally, 117
Funicello, Annette, 124,

127, 134
Furlong, "Pink," 104

G

Gehrig, Lou, 107
Ghana, 188
Gidget. *See* Kohner, Kathy.
Gidget (novel and movie), 124
Gidget Goes Hawaiian (movie), 124
Gidget Goes to Rome (movie), 124
Gifford, Frank, 130
Gilmore, Patricia, 95
  comments about Duke's initial surfing exhibition in Australia, 95
Good Relations clubs, 73
Grays Beach (Waikiki), 74
Griffin, Rick, 144
  posters by, *140, 141*
Gustaf, King (of Sweden), 89, 92
Gusti Putu Sana
  Balinese painting by, *186–187*

H

H.E.D. (*Honolulu Advertiser* writer)
  comments about Waikiki beachboys in a dance contest, 77
Hakman, Jeff, 162
Hakuole, Jimmy, *79*
Hale, Louis "Sally," 78
Haleiwa, 22–23
Halekulani Regent Hotel, 68
Hands-Around-the Pacific Club, 73
Hang Ten, 10
Harbord (Australia), 95
Harmony Park (Calif.), 134
Harris, Gay, 78
Harrison, Loren, 109
Hau Tree Inn. *See* Halekulani Regent Hotel.
Hawaii
  surfing in, 9, 10–11, 30, 33, 34, 37–38, 41, 43, 46, 49–52, 54
Hawaiian Annual (book)
  report about surfing, 34
The Hawaiian Archipelago, Six Months Among the Palm Groves, Coral Reefs, & Volcanoes of the Sandwich Islands (book), 52
Hawaiian Ethnological Notes, 54
"Hawaiian Hollow

Surfboard," 82
Hawaiian Surfboard (book), 82
Hawaiian Surfboard Paddling Championships, 82
Hawaiian Trail and Mountain Club, 73
Head, Bob, 191
Healani club, 77
Healy, Cecil
  comments about Duke surfing in Australia, 95
Hedemann, Hans, *18,* 154
he'e holua (coasting on a sled), 42
he'enalu (surfing), 30
  defined, 12
heiau (temple), 33
Hemmings, Fred, Jr. 98, *99,* 100, 162, 165
  comments about surfing contest winnings, 165
Henderson, Lew, 74
Hendrix, Jimi
  comments about surfing, 137
Hermosa Beach (Calif.), 118
Heublein Corporation, 162
Higgins, Delbert "Bud"
  comments about wooden surfboards, 107
hili (pounded bark of the *kukui*), 42
Hilo Bay (Hawaii), 52, *48, 56–57*
Ho, Michael, 154, 165
Hoffman, Philip "Flippy," 117, 133
Hoffman, Walter, 117, 133
Holland, Al, *108*
Hollinger, William, 78
Holmes, Burton, 73
Holmes, Paul
  comments about the traveling surfer, 198
Honolulu Opera House, 74
Ho'okena, 42
Hopkins, Jerry, 33
hōpūpū (state of being emotionally excited), 30
Horan, Cheyne, 154
Hossegor (southern France), *190–191*
Houston-Hawaii Surfing Week, 98
How to Stuff a Wild Bikini (movie), 124
Hui Nalu, 68, *71,* 77
  formation of, 74
Hunter, Tab, 130

Huntington, Henry E., 70, 105
Huntington Beach (Calif.), 98, *26*
Hutchinson, H., 107
Hynson, Mike, 146, 147, 188

I

Ii, John Papa
  comments about
    canoe leaping, 43
    Kaahumanu and Kamehameha surfing, 43
  surfing at Lahaina, 41
  types of surfboards, 41
Illinois Athletic Club, 97
The Illustrated London News (newspaper), 69
  surfing engraving in, *69*
Incidents of a Whaling Voyage (book), 51
International Professional Surfers (IPS), 165
International Surfing (magazine), 98
International Surfing Federation (ISF), 165
Iwa Class, 200

J

Jacobs, Harold "Hap," 114, 118
Japan, 165, 188, 195, *196–197, 197*
Jarvis, L., 107
Jan and Dean, 130, 136
Jeffrey's Bay (South Africa), *24–25*
"Jeux Haviens" (engraving by E. Riou), 52, *53*
Johnson, Bob, *108*

K

Kaahumanu, Queen, 42–43
Kahanamoku, Bill, 77
Kahanamoku, Duke Paoa, 73, *75,* 77, 78, *79,* 88, *89, 90, 91–92, 93,* 95–98, 100, *101,* 104, 162
  AAU swimming and diving meet in 1911, 88
  Tom Blake and, 81
  with the Boomerang Club in Australia, *94*
  comments about
    his ability to swim fast, 88
    his conversation with Jim Thorpe enroute to Stockholm Olympics, 91
  entering Olympic

competition at age 42, 98
  movie roles he played, 92
  the surf off Waikiki in summer of 1917, 96
  the victory wreath presented to him at the 1912 Stockholm Olympics by King Gustaf, 92
Elizabeth, Queen Mother of Great Britain and, 100
George Freeth and, 107
with Groucho Marx, *97*
the Hui Nalu and, 74
John Kennedy and, 100
Olympic trials swimming meet in 1912, 91
surfing, 92, 107
with his 1965 surf team, *99*
Kahanamoku, Sam, 97
"the Kahanamoku Kick," 91
kahuna (sorcerer), 30, 33
Kakioena, 38
Kala, Fat, 78
Kalakaua, 79
Kalanimoku, Chief, 35, 38
Kalamainu'u, 37
Ka-lani-'opuu, 38
Ka-lehua-weha, 37
Kaluhiokalani, Buttons, 22–23
Kamakau, Samuel Manaiakalani
  surfing myths recounted by, 37, 38
Kamakura (Japan), *196–197*
Kamana, Squeeze, 79
Kamehameha the Great, 42–43
Kampion, Drew
  comments about
    the short board, 153
    Nat Young's revolutionary surfing style, 153
"Ka Nalu" (chant), 12
Kaneamuna, Chiefess, 42
Kano, Clarence, 81
Kaumualii, 38
Kaupiko, Lukela "John D," 74
Kealakekua Bay (Hawaii), 49
Kealoha, Dane, 154
Kealoha, Pua, 75, 96
Keauokalani, Kepelino, 37
  comments about
    Ikuwā, 30
    surfing, 10
Keawenuiaumi, King, 42
Kechele, Matt, 20
Kerbox, Buzzy, 165,

194– 195
Kiha-a-Pii-lani, 37
kiki'o (type of surfboard), 41
King, Lieut. James, 49
  comments about
    first observing surfing, 49
    surfing at Kealakekua Bay,
    49
Kips Bay Theater (New
  York), 149
Kivlin, Matt, 111, 113, 114,
  116
Knox, Junior, 117
koa (a tree), 41
Kohner, Frederick "Fritz,"
  124
Kohner, Kathy, 124
Kolea-moku, 37
Kona (Hawaii), 52
Ku'emanu *(heiau),* 33
Kuhio, Prince, 74
Kuhio Beach, 68, 73, 78
Kuohu, 43
Kyushu (Japan), 188

L
La Bidassoa (France), 133
La Jolla (Calif.), 144
Laenihi, 33
Laguna Beach (Calif.), 114,
  118
Lahaina, 51
Landis, Hal, *108*
Laupahoehoe, 38
lele wa'a (canoe leaping), 43
Lembeck, Harvey, 127
Letham, Isabel, 95
"Let's Go Trippin" (song),
  134, 136
Levine, Larry, *24– 25*
*Life in the Sandwich Islands,
  The Heart of the Pacific, As
  It Was and Is* (book), 51
Lightning Bolt, 10
Liliuokalani, Queen, 74
Lindbergh, Larry, 98, 162
Lio-keo-keo (canoe), 74
Lippincott, Gardner, 109
London, Charmian, 68, 73
London, Jack, 68, 70, 73,
  77, 154
  comments about
    George Freeth, 70, 104
    surfing, 68
Lono-a-Piilani, 37
Lopez, Gerry, 77
Los Angeles Athletic Club,
  81, 107
**Los Angeles Ladder
  Company,** 82
Love, Turkey, 78
Lynch, Wayne, 165
Lyons, Splash, 78, *79*

M
**Mac Meda Destruction
  Company,** 134, 144
Macfarlane, Mrs. Walter, 74
MacGillivray, Greg, 133
Mackay, Wallis, 37
Mai-hiwa, 37
Maine, *28– 29*
Makaha (Hawaii), 117, 150,
  162, *177*
**Makaha International
  Surfing Championships,**
  114, 153
Makua, Blue, 78
Malibu (Calif.), 100, 111,
  115, 117, 124, *128– 129,*
  150
Manhattan (Calif.), 118
Manly Beach (Australia),
  153, 165
Marquesans, 49
Martin, "Lou," 104
Marx, Groucho
  with Duke Kahanamoku, *97*
Matavai Point (Tahiti), 46
Mauritius, 195
McAlister, Snowy, 95
  comments about Duke
    introducing surfing to
    Australia, 95
McClelland, Chuck, 117
McGillivray, Perry, 96
McQueen, Red
  comments about Duke's
    participation in the 1920
    Olympic Games, 96
McVay, Kimo Wilder, 98, 162
mele (chant), 33
Mid-Pacific Magazine, 73
Miller, Dudie. *See* Miller,
  Edward Kenneth
  Kaleleihealani.
Miller, Edward Kenneth
  Kaleleihealani (Dudie), *71,*
  74, 75
Minvielle, Toots, 78
"Miserlou" (song), 134, 136
missionaries
  influence of the — on
    surfing, 54
"Mister Pipeline." *See* Van
  'Artsdalen, Butch.
Mitchell, Warren, 191
Moana Bath House, 68
Moana Hotel, 68, 73, 74
Mokuahi, Sammy, Sr.
  ("Steamboat"), 78
mole ki (root of the ti plant),
  42
mo'o (serpent), 37
"Moondoggie," 124
Morocco, 188

Muñoz, Mickey, *125*
Murphy (cartoon character),
  144
Murphy, Jack "Murph the
  Surf," 144
Murray, Jim
  comments about Duke and
    John F. Kennedy, 100
Muscle Beach Party
  (movie), 122, 127, 128
Myrtle boat club, 73, 77
myth, dragon, 37

N
Narrabeen (Australia), 165
*Narrative of a Tour Through
  Hawaii* (book), 50
New Jersey, 165
New South Wales, 192
Newbreak (Calif.), 134
Newport Beach (Calif.), 97,
  148– 149, 181
Nha Trang (Vietnam), 195
Number Threes (Waikiki),
  68
Nupepa Kuokoa
  (newspaper), 38
Nuuanupahu, 38

O
Ocean Pacific (OP), 165
Oceanside (Calif.), 104
Offshore Pipeline Masters,
  165
"Olé-Las Olas!" (article), 188
Olmstead, Francis Allyn
  comments about
    Hawaiians surfing, 41, 52
    drawing of surfers by, *40*
'olo (type of surfboard), 35,
  41, *80, 83*
1912 **Olympics**
  (Stockholm), 91
Orange County (Calif.), 133
**The Outrigger Canoe
  Club,** *62– 63,* 68, 73– 74,
  77, 200
  formation of, 73

P
  Pacific Aquatic Carnival,
  95
**Pacific Coast Surf Board
  Championship** meet, 104,
  107
  First Annual, *83*
**Pacific Coast Surfriding
  Championship,** 82, 109
  See also Pacific Coast Surf
  Board Championship
  meet.
Pacific Electric Railway,
  104

Paiea, 38
Palos Verdes (Calif.), 104
Palos Verdes Surfing Club,
  108, 109
  ticket to a luau, *110*
Pan Pacific Union, 73
papa holua (land toboggan),
  42
Park, Sarah
  comments about
    Waikiki beachboys, 78
    surfers' lifestyle, 117
    Makaha as a new surf spot,
    117
Pasadena (Calif.), 111
Patterson, C. D., 92
Paul, Les, 134
Pearson, Hal, 108
Pelekane, 41
Pellion, Andrew, 34
Peru, 165, *193, 195*
Peterson, Michael, 165
Peterson, Preton "Pete," 109
petroglyphs, surfer
  at Kona, *31*
  at Lanai, *32*
Pezman, Steve
  comments about
    California-Hawaii surf
    connection, 117
    California surfers-turned-
    successful businessmen,
    133
    surfing, 10
The Philippines, 195
"Pink," 124
Pipeline Masters,
  160– 161, 162, *176*
Polynesian Researches
  (book), 38
polyurethane foam, 114,
  119, 124
Portugal, 195
Potter, Martin, 154
Pua'a (North Kona, Hawaii),
  43
Puerto Rico, 165
Pump House (Calif.), 134
The Pump House Gang
  (book), 144, 146
Puna'i-koae'e, 37

Q
quasimodo, *125*
Queen Emma Estate, 73
Quigg, Joe, 111, 113, 114,
  116, 119
  comments about
    Matt Kivlin and small, light
    boards, 113– 114
    Bob Simmons, 111, 113
    Leslie Williams and Kivlin's
    surfing style, 115

R
Racism in surfing, 198
Radio 2SM, 162
Rarick, Randy, 165
Rawlins, William F., 74
Redondo Breakwater
  (Calif.), photo of, *126– 127,
  178*
Redondo (Calif.), 104, 105,
  118
**Redondo-Los Angeles
  Railway,** 70
Reid, Sam
  comments about Tom
    Blake's hollow surfboard,
    82
Reidelberger, Fran
  interviews Duke, 68
Rendezvous Ballroom
  (Calif.), 134
Resolution (ship), 49
Reynolds, Wade
  painting by, *145*
Richards, Mark, 154, *164*
Ride the Wild Surf (movie),
  123, 130
Rincon (Calif.), *27*
Riou, E., 52
Rip Curl, 162
Riverside (Calif.), 134
Robello, Harry, *79*
Rochlen, Dave, 113, 114
  comments about
    Bob Simmons, 111
    surfing, 10
    Joe Quigg and, 111
Rogers, Art, *108*
Rosegg, Peter
  comments about the
    Sammy "Steamboat"
    Mokuahi, Sr. Waikiki
    Beachboy Festival, 81
Ross, Norman, 96
Roughing It (book), 52
"A Royal Sport: Surfing at
  Waikiki" (article), 68
Ruling Chiefs of Hawaii
  (book), 38
Russell, Rory, *176, 193*

S
"Salute to Hawaii"
  (promotion/tour), 100
**Sammy "Steamboat"
  Mokuahi, Sr. Waikiki
  Beachboy Festival,** 78
San Clemente (Calif.), 118,
  133
San Diego, 118, 153, 165
San Miguel (Baja Calif.),
  134
San Onofre, 109, 118

San Quintin (Baja Calif.), *199*

Santa Monica Bay (Calif.), 104

Santa Monica Beach (Calif.), 98, 109, 111, 113

Santa Monica Civic Auditorium, 134, 147

Severson, John, 130, 133

The Seychelles, 195

Shank, Bud, 146

sharks
  in surf legends, 38

Sharp, Bill, *148– 149*

Shingle, Mrs. Robert W., 74

Shipley, Jack, 165

"Silver Surfer" (comic book), *146*

Simmons, Bob, 111, 113, 114

skeg, 107, 109

"Slantcher" (surfboard, *also* "Slantwise"), 109

"Slantwise" (surfboard), 109

Slippery When Wet (movie), 146

Smart, Mrs. Henry G., 74

Smirnoff Pro-Am meet, 162

South Africa, 165, 195, 197

Spain, 133, 188

Spreckles, A. Bunker, *152*

Steadman, Ralph
  drawings by, *142, 143*

"Steamboat." *See* Mokuahi, Sr., Sammy.

Steel, Ned, 74

Stoddard, William, 50
  comments about surfing, 37

Stokes, John Francis Gray, 33

Straight Talk Tyres Open, 165

Strauch, Paul, Jr., 98, *99,* 100
  comments about surfing, 9

styrofoam in surfboards, 111, 113

Summer Cruising in the South Seas (book), 37, *50*
  engraving from, *36*

Sunkist World Cup meet, 165

Sunn, Rell, *183*

Sunset Beach (Hawaii), 98

"Supertubes" (South Africa), *24– 25*

Surf Classics (movie), 134

Surf Guide (magazine), 188

"surf music," 127, 130, 134, 136, 137, 210– 215

surf ski, *155*

The Surfaris, 134

surfboard(s), 113, 154, *158– 159*
  oldest *known,* 42
  olo, 35, 80, 83
  short style, 153
  of the 1800's, 41, 52
  first in Australia, 92
    with colorful designs, 113
    with concave bottoms, 111
    fiberglass finned, 113
    hollow, 81– 82, 107
    illustrated, 49
    polyurethane foam, 114
    "Sandwich Boards," 111
    small, light, 113

Surfboarding in Oceania: Its Pre-European Distribution (article), 34

"surfbuilding ritual," 41

Surfer (magazine), 10, 130, *132, 133,* 188

Surfing (magazine), 133

surfing contests, 162, 165
  in Bali, 191, 195
  in California, 82, 107, 109, 114
  in Hawaii, 98, 114, 165
  in South Africa, 165, 195, 197, 198

Surfing Hall of Fame, 98

Surfing Hollow Days (movie), 134

Surfline Hawaii, 10

Swastika Surfboard Company, 9

Swedson, Clyde, 107

Sweet, Dave, 114

Swimming Hall of Fame, 98

T

Tahitians, 46, 49

tandem surfing, *65,* 124

Tate, Sharon, 127

Thelma (yacht), 97

Thomas N. Rogers Company, 82

Thomson, Shaun, 154

Thorpe, Jim, 91

Tilley, Ian, 191

Toffler, Alvin
  comments about the surfing lifestyle, 156

Tom Morey Invitational "noseriding" contest, 162

Torgerson, Dial
  comments about Duke's role as a Hollywood actor and real life hero, 97

Torrance, Dean, 136

"Tough Bill," 77

Townend, Peter, 165

Traditions of Hawaii (book), 30

The Trashmen, 136

Trent, Buzzy, 111, 117

Trestles (Oceanside, Calif.), *155*

"Tubesteak," 124

Tucker, Cliff, *108,* 109
  comments about
    surfing then and now, 109
    West Coast surfers in the 1930s and 1940s, 109
    winning the 1940 meet at San Onofre, 109

Twain, Mark, *51*
  comments about
    his attempt at surfing, 52
    Hawaiians surfing, 52

2SM/Coca-Cola Bottlers Surf-about, 165

U

Ua Nuka (movie), 92

Uluwatu (Bali, Indonesia), 188, *192*

Umi, 38

United States Surfing Championship, 98

Unulau (trade wind), 33

Uranie (ship), 34

Uruguay, 188

V

Van Artsdalen, Butch, 99, 100

Vance, "Dazzy," 107

Velzy, Dale, 114, 118

Venice (Calif.), *102– 103,* 118

Ventura (CaLif.), 162

The Ventures, 136

Vietnam, 195

Vogue (magazine)
  surfing cover shot in, *85*

A Voyage Round the World (book), 50

A Voyage to the Pacific Ocean (book), 49

Vultee, Art, 107

Vultee, Gerrard, 107

Vung Tau (Vietnam), 195

W

Waikiki, 37, *64, 65,* 68, 70, 73, 77, 96, 118
  surfing at *55, 58– 59, 60– 61*

Waikiki Surf Club, 153
  See also Waikiki Swimming Club.

Waikiki Swimming Club (later known as Waikiki Surf Club), 68

Waimau, J.
  comments about men and women surfers of 1865, 38

Waimea Bay (Hawaii), *14– 15,* 130, *166– 167*

The Wake of the Red Witch (movie), 92

Warriewood (Australia), 165

water polo, 105

Watson, Keller, 109

Wayne, John, 92

Weber, Dewey, 114

Webber, John, 49
  drawing of Kealakekua by, *44– 45,* 47

Weismuller, Johnny, 97, 98

Wilcox, Ella Wheeler, 73

wiliwili (breadfruit tree), 41

Williams, Leslie, 113, 114

Williams, R., 107

Williams, "Sid," 104

Wilson, Brian, 130, 136

Windansea (Calif.), 114, 118

Windansea Surf Club, 135

windsurfing, 11, 200, *201*

Winter, Kenneth, 74

Wolfe, Tom, 144, 146
  comments about the future of surfing, 146

World Contest, 153

Y

Yater, Reynolds, 114

Young, Robert "Nat," 153, 162

The Young Wave Hunters (movie), 134

Z

Zahn, Tom, 114, *116, 119*

Zamboanga Bar (Los Angeles), *108*

Zeller, Bernie, *108*

Zuckerman, Kathy. *See* Kohner, Kathy.

CREDITS

Cover: Aaron Chang.

Frontispiece:"Surfing at Hilo Bay," ca. 1850; detail from an oil painted on a biscuit tin; artist unknown; from the collection of Mr. and Mrs. Don Severson, Honolulu.

8 — "Surf Rider," ca. 1890, by Theodore P. Severin; from the Bernice Pauahi Bishop Museum, Honolulu.

11 — Jeff Divine/*Surfer*.

13 — Steve Wilkings/*Surfer*.

14— Denjiro Sato/*Surfer*.

—17 — Warren Bolster/*Surfer*.

18 — Craig Fineman/*Surfer*.

19 — Peter Crawford/*Surfer*.

20 — Darrell Jones/*Surfer*.

21—23 — Steve Wilkings/*Surfer*.

24—25 — Jeff Divine/*Surfer*.

26 — John Lyman/*Surfer*.

27 — Jimmy Metyko/*Surfer*.

28—29 — Stephen O. Muskie/*Surfer*.

31—32 — Edward Stasack.

35 — Jacques Arago and Andrew Pellion (engraver); from the collection of Mr. and Mrs. Don Severson.

36 — Wallis Mackay; from *Summer Cruising in the South Seas*, 1874.

39 — From The Hawaiian Historical Society.

40 — Francis Allyn Olmsted, from *Incidents of a Whaling Voyage*, 1841; from the collection of Mr. and Mrs. Don Severson.

44—45 — John Webber; from the collection of David Eith.

47 — John Webber (detail); from the collection of David Eith.

48 — "Surfing at Hilo Bay," ca. 1850; an oil painted on a biscuit tin; artist unknown; from the collection of Mr. and Mrs. Don Severson.

50 — Wallis Mackay; from *Summer Cruising in the South Seas* (cover), 1874.

51 — From *Roughing It* by Mark Twain, 1866; from the collection of David Eith.

53 — "Jeux Haviens," by E. Riou; from *Qatorze Ans Aux Iles Sandwich*; from the collection of Mr. and Mrs. Don Severson.

55 — Frank Davey, ca. 1900; from the Bernice Pauahi Bishop Museum.

56—57 — Surfers at Hilo Bay, ca. 1900; photographer unknown; from the Bishop Museum.

58—59 — Charles William Bartlett, ca. 1920; from the Honolulu Academy of Arts.

60—61 — Surfers at Waikiki, ca. 1920s; photographer unknown; from the Hawaii State Archives.

62—63 — The Hawaii State Archives.

64 — From the collection of Warren Johnston.

65 — The Associated Press.

66 — From the collection of Gordon McClelland.

67 — From the collection of Leonard Lueras.

69 — J. Begg, *The Illustrated London News*, 1910; from the collection of Dr. N. Fred Meyers.

70 — Ray Jerome Baker; of Mrs. Willis Marks, 1912; from the Bernice Pauahi Bishop Museum.

71—7 — Ray Jerome Baker; from the Bernice Pauahi Bishop Museum.

75 — Hal Prieste; courtesy of Herb Wetenkamp III.

76 — Courtesy of Alexander & Baldwin Inc.; hand-coloring by Steve Shrader.

79 — From the collection of Waltah Clarke.

80 — From the Bernice Pauahi Bishop Museum.

83 — From the Hawaiian Historical Society.

84 — Courtesy of Alexander & Baldwin Inc.; from the collection of Gordon McClelland.

85 — Toni Frissell; reproduced courtesy of *Vogue*, The Condé Nast Publications Inc., and the Library of Congress.

86—87 — From the Bernice Pauahi Bishop Museum.

89 — From the collection of Kimo Wilder McVay.

90-L — From the Bernice Pauahi Bishop Museum.

90-R — Robert A. Bonine; from the collection of Dr. Fred N. Meyers.

93—99 — News of Hawaii photo; from the collection of Kimo Wilder McVay.

101 — Ron Stoner/*Surfer*.

102—103 — From the collection of Dr. N. Fred Meyers.

105 — Tom Coyner.

106 — From the Hawaiian Historical Society.

10 — From the collection of Cliff Tucker.

110 — Art Rogers photo; from the collection of Cliff Tucker.

112 — Courtesy of John Heath "Doc" Ball; from *California Surfriders*, 1946, 1979.

115—119 — From the collection of Ricky Grigg.

120—121 — "Decals In Excess," 1983, by Jim Evans; a woodie still life from the collection of Leonard Lueras.

122 — American International Pictures.

123 — Columbia Pictures.

125 — John Severson; from the collection of *Surfer* magazine.

126—127 — Art Rogers of the *Los Angeles Times*; from the collection of Otis and Norman Chandler.

128—129 — From the collection of *Surfer* magazine.

131 — Leroy Grannis; from the collection of *Surfer* magazine.

132 — John Severson; from the collection of *Surfer* magazine.

135 — Ron Stoner/*Surfer*.

137 — Poster design by John Van Hammersveld for *The Endless Summer*; from the collection of Gordon McClelland.

138—139 — Photograph courtesy of Zoetrope Studios. Copyright 1979 by Omni Zoetrope. All Rights Reserved.

140 — Rick Griffin; original artwork for the film *Five Summer Stories*, 1979, by MacGillivray-Freeman Films.

141 — Rick Griffin; original artwork for the film *Blazing Boards*, 1983, by Chris Bystrom.

142—143 — Ralph Steadman, 1981.

14 — "Young Man With Surfboard," 1971; oil on canvas by Wade Reynolds; reproduced courtesy of the Louis Newman Galleries, Beverly Hills, California; from the collection of Otis Chandler.

146 — "The Silver Surfer"; courtesy of the Marvel Comics Group. All rights reserved.

147 — "Surfer"; original air-brush art by Jim Evans.

148—149 — Mike Moir/*Surfer*.

150—151 — Jeff Divine/*Surfer*.

152 — Art Brewer/*Surfer*.

155 — Jeff Divine/*Surfer*.

157 — Chuck Schmid/*Surfer*.

158—159 — Tom Servais photos of original surfboard art.

160—161 — Jeff Divine/*Surfer*.

163 — K. Wilkes/*Surfer*.

164 — Rob Hutchinson/*Surfer*.

166—167 — Steve Wilkings/*Surfer*.

169 — A. Debutiaco/*Surfer*.

170—171 — Jim Russi/*Surfer*.

172—173 — Dan Merkel/*Surfer*.

174 — Alan Rich/*Surfer*.

175 — Steve Wilkings/*Surfer*.

176 — Warren Bolster/*Surfer*.

177 — Steve Wilkings/*Surfer*.

178 — Jim Cassimus/*Surfer*.

179 — Jeff Divine/*Surfer*.

180 — Dennis Junor/*Surfer*.

181 — Steve Sakamoto/*Surfer*.

182—183 — Jeff Divine/*Surfer*.

184—185 — Jimmy Metyko/*Surfer*.

186—187 — I. Gusti Putu Sana; Chinese ink on canvas; Detail vignette by I. Made Budi; from the collection of Leonard Lueras.

189 — I. Made Budi; Chinese ink and water color; from the collection of Leonard Lueras.

190—191 — Jeff Divine/*Surfer*.

192 — Jim Russi/*Surfer*.

193—195 — Darrell Jones/*Surfer*.

196—197 — Greg Davis.

199 — Aaron Chang/*Surfing*.

201 — Steve Wilkings.

203 — Wayne Levin.

204—209 — Templature by Dick DeLong.

210—215 — Photo copies by Tom Servais; from *Surfer* magazine.

216 — Ray Jerome Baker photo of the filmmaker Robert A. Bonine; from the Bishop Museum.

222 — Wayne Levin.

228 — "Murphy," 1983, by Rick Griffin.

235 — Peter French.

Back Cover: Stephen O. Muskie/*Surfer*.

ACKNOWLEDGMENTS

Before bailing out, I would like to personally thank some of the individuals and institutions who contributed in so many different ways to the creation of this book. Chief among these associates and contributors were Fred Bechlen, who prepared the book's master design grid and spent many late nights fine-tuning its typographical and graphical elements; Nedra, my chief editor, conscience and wife, who read all manuscripts carefully, prepared the index, and, most important, gave me endless solace and moral support throughout the book-making process; Sandy Zalburg, who unmercifully read and edited preliminary manuscripts; Steve Shrader, who offered a good design eye and/or a late night drink when either/or was needed; and Steve Wilkings and Jeff Divine, who early on contributed invaluable advice and "technical" assistance.

Also important were librarians and archivists from the Bernice Pauahi Bishop Museum, the University of Hawaii's Hamilton Library, the Hawaii State Archives, the Hawaiian Historical Society, the Honolulu Academy of Arts, the Hawaiian Mission Children's Society, *The Honolulu Advertiser, The Honolulu Star-Bulletin, Honolulu Magazine, The Los Angeles Times, The Santa Ana Daily Register, The San Diego Tribune,* The Academy of Motion Picture Arts and Sciences and the Library of Congress. Additional archival assistance was also cordially offered by The Condé Nast Publications Inc. (New York), Zoetrope Studios (San Francisco and Hollywood), the Marvel Comics Group (New York) and the Louis Newman Galleries (Beverly Hills). Individuals who contributed the use of works in their private collections included Mr. and Mrs. Don Severson, Dr. Fred N. Meyers, Dr. David T. Eith, Kimo McVay, Cliff Tucker, Ricky Grigg, Waltah Clarke, Warren Johnston, past members of the California Western University Surfing Association, Alexander and Baldwin Inc., Dr. John Heath "Doc" Ball, Bank Wright, Gordon McClelland, Rick Griffin, Jim Evans and Norman and Otis Chandler.

Individual photographers are credited on the opposite page, but a special *mahalo* plenty to Steve Pezman, publisher, and Jeff Divine, photo editor, who graciously gave me permission to use early and contemporary works on file in the *Surfer* magazine photo archive/agency. The *Surfer* collection has to be the most valuable and complete in the world of modern surfing, and from it came many of this book's most stunning and historically important visuals.

For their help in gathering data published in the book's appendices section, thank you to Barry Morrison for compiling bibliographical matters; Dick DeLong for his template renderings in the section on evolution of the surfboard; Tino Ramirez for collecting above- and underground matters that became our surf filmography; and Jennifer Chu, who edited and retyped all these "scholarly" bits and pieces.

Time, energy and advice were also contributed by the late Duke Kahanamoku, Dave Rochlen, Joe Quigg, George Downing, Paul Strauch, Fred Hemmings, Randy Rarick, Doug Godfrey, John Grissim, Neal Izumi, Peter Wong, Jerry Hopkins, Joe Feher, Barbara Dunn, Betty Kam, Debbie Dunn, Henk Kuiper (of Master Color Laboratories), Mike Macintyre and John Hooper (of the British Broadcasting Corporation), Tom Coyner, Zenia Cleigh, Paul Holmes, Jim Kempton, Rus Calisch (of *The Surf Report*), Peggy Bendet, Elliott Almond, Grady Timmons, Ronn Ronck, John White, Bill Tucker, Abner Stein, Leo Haks, Baron Wolman, Greg Davis, Carol Uyeda, Vernie Miner, Kazuko Inoue, Rodney Lim, Dennis Young, Rene Kitagawa, Josie Herr, Wendy Chong, Paul Tomatani, Rick Smolan, David Cohen, Peter Workman, Suzanne Rafer, Wayne Kirn, Osam Kobayashi, Hiromi Ohno, Tina Yu, Kris Sam and many others.

Very special mention, however, must be made of the many personal and "logistical" contributions made by Tom Chapman of Emphasis, Inc., Tokyo, and Steve Ellis of Emphasis (Hong Kong) Ltd. Without them this latest publishing wave might never have broken. Another Emphasis colleague who *made it all possible was* Elvis Loo, Emphasis-Hong Kong's production chief, who carefully steered the book through its final and painstaking production phases. Other Emphasis people who helped with production matters included Kumar Pereira, Stephen Ma, Samuel Lau and Nolan Tam.

A belated thank you to my parents, Leo and Mela, who many years ago gave me the money I needed to buy my first surfboard, but finally — and ultimately — a sincere *me ke aloha pumehana* to the ancients of Polynesia who discovered, enjoyed and refined this wonderful and special pleasure we call surfing.

— Leonard Lueras,
Honolulu,
Oahu, Hawaii
March, 1984

Leonard Lueras left the mainland for Hawaii in 1963 because he wanted to ride better and bigger waves. He still surfs, but now spends most of his time as an editor and journalist specializing in topics relating to the Pacific and Far East. Lueras is the editorial director of Emphasis International, an Asia-based magazine and book publishing group. He lives in Honolulu's Manoa Valley.